TOUCHED BY THE GREAT PHYSICIAN

AN ACCOUNT OF DIVINE HEALING

Jo,

May our Lord richly touch & bless your life!

Love & Prayers,

TOUCHED BY THE GREAT PHYSICIAN

AN ACCOUNT OF DIVINE HEALING

GUY L. MYERS

WINEPRESS WP PUBLISHING

© 1999 by Guy L. Myers. All rights reserved

Printed in the United States of America

Packaged by WinePress Publishing, PO Box 428, Enumclaw, WA 98022. The views expressed or implied in this work do not necessarily reflect those of WinePress Publishing. Ultimate design, content, and editorial accuracy of this work are the responsibilities of the author.

No part of this publication may be reproduced, stored in a retrieval system, or transmitted in any way by any means—electronic, mechanical, photocopy, recording, or otherwise—without the prior permission of the copyright holder, except as provided by USA copyright law.

Unless otherwise noted all scriptures are taken from the Holy Bible, New King James Version, Copyright © 1979, 1980, 1982 by Thomas Nelson, Inc., Publishers. Used by permission.

ISBN 1-57921-192-5
Library of Congress Catalog Card Number: 99-63454

This book is dedicated to the honor and glory of the Lord Jesus Christ and to the furtherance of His gospel. Proceeds above expenses received from this book will be used to bring hope and encouragement to others.

Acknowledgments

There are numerous people to whom I want to express my appreciation and thanksgiving. Our Heavenly Father expressed His love for Marilyn and me through them all.

I first want to express my thanks and appreciation to my parents, Arlo and Lois Myers. They introduced me to the Lord Jesus Christ at a very young age and taught me to put my faith and trust in Him. Thanks, Mom and Dad, for raising me in a Christian environment and for your never-ending love and support.

A special thanks to both my and Marilyn's entire families and all our many friends for your prayers, love, and support. You all are special and dear to us.

I want to thank the many congregations and individuals in Johnstown, Pennsylvania and across the country who were constantly praying for Marilyn's healing. Many of you we have never met, yet you prayed for Marilyn's healing. May God richly bless you all, and may your faith in Him increase.

Acknowledgments

I want to express my appreciation to each doctor and nurse who attended to Marilyn during her prolonged hospitalization in Pittsburgh and Johnstown, Pennsylvania. Thanks for your love and concern.

I especially want to express my appreciation to the congregation that I pastor, the Conemaugh Church of the Brethren. Thanks for all your love and concern and for allowing me to spend time with Marilyn during her prolonged hospitalization. Every pastor should be blessed to have a congregation as special as you.

I want to thank all of the wonderful neighbors that Marilyn and I are blessed to live beside. I especially want to thank Willard and Beryl for tending the mail and for the delicious meals when I was able to be home. Thanks to "Big Rude" and Mary for tending my lawn and for the delicious meals. Thanks to Luella and Margaret for making the delicious tomato juice from the tomatoes in our garden. And thanks to all for your many prayers, cards, and words of comfort.

I also want to express my appreciation to two special friends, Andrea Thompson and Craig Stoner, for their editing skills, spiritual insight and encouragement.

Above all, I thank my Lord and Savior Jesus Christ for being faithful to His Word. He truly is the Good Shepherd and the Great Physician.

Contents

Contents

Introduction

There are seven redemptive names of Jesus Christ recorded in the Word of God. These seven names reveal Jesus as meeting every need of man.

The following are the seven redemptive names:

1. JEHOVAH-SHAMMAH: "The Lord is There," or "The Lord is Present," revealing to us the redemptive privilege of enjoying His presence. Jesus said, "Lo, I am with you always."
2. JEHOVAH-SHALOM: "The Lord our Peace." Jesus said, "My peace I give unto you."
3. JEHOVAH-RA-AH: "The Lord is my Shepherd." He became our Shepherd by giving "His life for the sheep."
4. JEHOVAH-JIREH: "The Lord will provide." Jesus Christ was the offering provided for our complete redemption.
5. JEHOVAH-NISSI: "The Lord is our Banner," or "The Lord is our Victor." By the cross, Jesus Christ triumphed over

principalities and powers. "Thanks be unto God who gives us the victory through our Lord Jesus Christ" (I Cor. 15:57).

6. JEHOVAH-TSIDKENU: "The Lord our Righteousness." He became our righteousness by bearing our sins on the cross. We receive the gift of righteousness by having faith in Christ.

7. JEHOVAH-RAPHA: "I am the Lord thy Physician," or "I am the Lord that heals you."

God revealed Himself as our Physician in the very first covenant He gave after He used Moses to miraculously lead His people through the Red Sea. "And He said, 'If you diligently heed the voice of the Lord your God and do what is right in His sight, give ear to His commandments and keep all His statutes, I will put none of the diseases on you which I have brought on the Egyptians. For I am the Lord who heals you'" (Exod. 15:26).

This is not only a promise. It is a statute and an ordinance. "Is anyone among you sick? Let him call for the elders of the church, and let them pray over him, anointing him with oil in the name of the Lord" (James 5:14).

To Those Who Need Healing

Jesus said, "The Word is the seed" (Luke 8:11). It is the seed of divine life. Until the person seeking healing is sure from God's Word that it is God's will to heal him, he is trying to reap a harvest where there is no seed planted. It would be impossible for a farmer to have faith for a harvest before he was sure the seed had been planted.

For one to say, "I believe the Lord is able to heal me" before he knows from God's Word that He is willing to heal him is like a farmer saying, "I believe God is able to give me a harvest" without any seed being planted or watered.

Seed is powerless until it is planted. Instead of saying, "Pray for me," many should first say, "Teach me God's Word so that I can intelligently cooperate for my recovery." We must know what the benefits of Calvary are before we can appropriate them by faith. David specifies, "Bless the Lord, O my soul, And forget not all His benefits: Who forgives all your iniquities, who heals all your diseases" (Ps. 103:2–3).

After we have been enlightened, our attitude toward sickness should be the same as our attitude toward sin. Our purpose to have our bodies healed should be as definite as our purpose to have our souls healed. That purpose is to give honor and glory to the Lord Jesus Christ.

Between the time we definitely commit the healing of our bodies to God, and the completion of our healing, we should learn one of the most valuable lessons of the Christian life. That lesson is how to observe Hebrews 10:35–36: "Therefore do not cast away your confidence, which has great reward. For you have need of endurance, so that after you have done the will of God, you may receive the promise."

Marilyn and I are extremely grateful to all who help us to endure and persevere.

The Evidence of Things Not Seen

After you have planted your seed, you must believe it is growing before you will see it grow. This is the faith that is "the evidence of things not seen." In Christ, we have perfect evidence for faith. Any man or woman can get rid of their doubts by looking steadfastly and only at the evidence which God has given for faith. Seeing only what God says will produce and increase faith.

1

The Lord Is My Shepherd

On April 28, 1998, Marilyn and I celebrated our twenty-fifth wedding anniversary. The evening before, we agreed to spend our special day out of town. We did not make any reservations at a restaurant or a motel. We thought that we would just "go with the flow."

However, at 7:30 A.M. on our special day, the telephone rang as we were eating breakfast. Someone from our congregation asked to meet with me that morning at my study. She was seeking guidance for her life and wanted someone to talk to. I agreed to meet with her at 10:00 A.M. After all, I thought that's what any good shepherd of his congregation would do.

Just as we finished our session, the telephone rang in my study. Another person from our congregation needed some encouragement and advice. Our telephone conversation lasted for about an hour.

By the time I returned home for lunch it was 12:30 P.M. During lunch, Marilyn and I learned that Peggy, a longtime faithful member of our church, had just been admitted to a local hospital. As she was walking to a grocery store near her home, she tripped on the sidewalk and landed face down. She had several injuries that needed to be treated. Marilyn and I agreed that I needed to go to the hospital to have prayer with her. After all, I thought that's what any good shepherd of his congregation would do.

When I returned home, Marilyn and I agreed that we would go to a local restaurant for a quiet dinner together. When we returned home, Marilyn gave me a very special anniversary gift. It was a copy of the Twenty-third Psalm, "The Lord is My Shepherd," surrounded by a beautiful silver frame. I know the Twenty-third Psalm very well, and I knew that the Lord Jesus was my Shepherd. At least, I thought I did. When Marilyn gave me that beautiful gift, I felt that God was speaking to me, but I did not know exactly what He was saying at that time.

A few days later, May 4, Marilyn and I spent the entire day at Children's Hospital in Pittsburgh, Pennsylvania, with a faithful family of our congregation, Beth and Dave and Beth's parents, Don and Pat. Beth and Dave's two-year-old son, Blake, needed corrective surgery on his aorta. The artery was blocked.

After the surgery, the surgeon told the family that there had been an opening in his aorta only as big as a pinhead. Praise God, the surgery went very well, and their son was in church the following Sunday. A few days before the young boy's surgery, I said to his mother, "This is another test for you." A few weeks before their son's surgery, Dave and Beth were involved in an auto accident. While their vehicle was in the shop waiting to be repaired, I told Beth that this whole process was a test. Little did I know the test that Marilyn and I were about to experience a few hours after we returned home from Pittsburgh that night.

Marilyn and I returned home about 5:30 P.M. Marilyn made a delicious supper that night consisting of fresh walleyes—which I had caught a few days before—macaroni salad, and a vegetable. After supper, we watched the day's local and national newscasts on television and then went to bed about 9:00 P.M. Before getting in bed, Marilyn said to me, "How about unplugging the telephone in our bedroom?" We were expecting some phone calls, and she did not want the ringing telephone to awaken her. There are two other phones in our house that would ring.

I said, "What if there is an emergency?"

Marilyn said, "There's not going to be an emergency. Please unplug the phone in our room." And so I did because I could tell that she was very tired. I believe that we both went to sleep as soon as our bodies hit the mattress. At approximately 12:30 A.M. I was awakened by a strange noise. It was Marilyn. She had apparently had some type of a seizure. She was lifeless. Immediately I tried to call 911 from our bedroom, but the phone was dead. I went to another room to get our portable phone and then called 911.

The dispatcher told me to get Marilyn out of bed and to put her on the floor. When I did that, I really believed at that time that she had died. I was petrified. As the 911 dispatcher was giving me instructions, I realized that Marilyn was breathing. I continued to do what the dispatcher told me to until the paramedics arrived. When I arrived at the hospital about thirty minutes later, I did not know what condition Marilyn was in. It was difficult waiting to be able to see her. When I finally was able to see her, she was awake and alert. Marilyn did not have a clue as to what had happened. All she knew was that she went to bed a few hours earlier in her own bedroom, and awoke in the emergency room of the hospital surrounded by people in blue paramedic suits.

During her three-day hospital stay, Marilyn was told that she had kidney damage, that she apparently had some type of a seizure, and also that a chord holding one of her heart valves in place was torn (chordae tendonini, pro lapse mitro valve). When Marilyn's doctor told me about the torn chord I asked, "Does this require surgery?"

The doctor said, "No, not now, but perhaps in a year or two." Marilyn was given a prescription for the seizing, and she also was given a new blood-pressure medication. (She began taking blood-pressure medication in 1985.) In about two weeks, she broke out in a terrible rash that began at the base of her neck. Her doctor said that either the seizure drug or the new blood-pressure medication was causing the rash. She apparently was allergic to one or both of them. The doctor finally changed both of the medications. Marilyn was prescribed another seizure medication. She did not tolerate that one very well at all. She would become dizzy and nauseous. After a few weeks of bloodwork and adjusting the dosage, Marilyn finally seemed to be getting back to being herself.

From the time Marilyn was hospitalized, I was a very anxious and worried preacher. I wasn't eating properly, I was making a lot more mistakes than usual, and I just wasn't myself. One day during that time, I was about to enter a local grocery store when an acquaintance of mine was just exiting the store. Rosie works at a local office supply store. She has a very bubbly personality and always has something good to say. As she spotted me she said, "Oh, Pastor Myers, it's so good to see you. How are you doing?"

I said, "I'm not doing very well today."

She said, "Oh, what's wrong?"

I then told her about Marilyn's physical problems. Tears came to her eyes, and she said, "Pastor, let me tell you about my concerns." She then told me about her father's recent stroke, which left him physically impaired in some ways. She told me about one of her sisters that was just recently diagnosed with cancer. And then she told me about another sister that was a diabetic. With tears in her eyes she said, "Pastor, I think we both need a hug today." As we were hugging and crying in that store parking lot, she said to me, "Oh, Pastor, isn't it good that we have Jesus to turn to?"

At that very moment, the Lord brought to my mind that beautiful twenty-fifth wedding anniversary present that Marilyn gave to me, the Twenty-third Psalm in a silver frame, "The Lord is My Shepherd." I said, "Yes, Rosie. It is good that we have Jesus to turn to."

As I entered the grocery store that day, I knew then what God was trying to say to me when Marilyn gave me that special gift. I wasn't allowing Jesus to be my Shepherd. I was trying to take care of Marilyn myself. I wasn't allowing the Great Physician to doctor her. I wasn't applying God's Word to her situation. That truth hit me like a ton of bricks. I asked myself, *Why am I worrying? Why have I not given her completely over to Jesus? Why am I not trusting in Jesus to bring healing to Marilyn? I trust Him to meet the needs of the*

people in my congregation when I pray with them. Why am I
not trusting in Jesus to meet the needs of my wife?

One of the ways that God speaks to me is through music.
The Holy Spirit reminded me of the words to a special song:

> Give up, and let Jesus take over.
> Give up, and let Jesus take over.
> And He'll make a way for you.
> Well, if you got mountains that you can't climb,
> If you got a river that you can't cross,
> And if you got a valley that you can't span,
> Let Jesus, let Jesus hold your hand.
> If you got burdens too hard to bear,
> If your load is more than your share,
> Kneel down and talk to Jesus.
> I know He cares.
> He'll make a way somehow.*

As I was grocery shopping, I met Beth in an aisle. (Beth is
the person that I told a few weeks earlier that she was going
through a test.) Beth asked me about Marilyn. God knew
that I needed someone like Beth from our congregation to
talk to. I cried on her shoulder. Beth turned to me and said,
"Pastor, I think this is a test. Isn't that what you told me?"

I said, "Yes, Beth, you are correct. This is a test, and I
am going to pass it." From that day on I fully committed
Marilyn to Jesus. I wanted the Lord Jesus to really be my
Shepherd. I knew in my mind that the Good Shepherd
would bring security, peace, strength, guidance, and assurance to my life. I also knew that the Lord Jesus could heal
her. The Holy Spirit reminded of God's Word, "Therefore
He is also able to save to the uttermost those who come to

---

* By Howard Goodman.
  Copyright © 1957 by Cedarwood Publishing.
  Used by permission.

God through Him, since He always lives to make intercession for them" (Heb. 7:25).

The Holy Spirit also reminded me of our Easter Sunday morning worship service on April 12, 1998. I had our congregation write their prayer concerns on index cards. I then invited them to come to the front of the church and have those needs nailed to a cross. I reminded our congregation that the Lord Jesus ever lives to make intercession for them. I also placed a card on that cross that Easter morning. One of my written concerns was physical healing for my wife, Marilyn. She just hadn't been feeling right during that time. She had been losing weight, and her appetite was very poor. That was a very moving part of the worship service. I could really sense the presence of God there that day. Now I understood why.

On Monday, July 6, 1998, Marilyn was told by her doctor that she was permitted to drive again. Marilyn continued to improve throughout the summer months. By the time Labor Day weekend arrived, Marilyn was very active. We went to several art-and-craft festivals that were in town that weekend. On Sunday, September 6, Marilyn said to me, "I really feel good. I haven't felt this good in a long time." She also seemed fine to me the next day, Labor Day. On Tuesday, September 8, Marilyn had a doctor's appointment. Her blood pressure was very high in the doctor's office. The doctor prescribed an additional blood-pressure medication that day.

When we awakened the next morning, I knew that something was very wrong. Marilyn looked very pale and somewhat dazed. I said to her, "Marilyn, are you feeling all right?" She told me that she had a bad headache. When we sat down to eat breakfast, I encouraged her to take her blood-pressure medication immediately.

After she took her medication, she told me that she was having visual problems. She also said that her vision was blurred at times on her right side. I called her neurologist, and he was able to see Marilyn that afternoon. After he examined her, he said, "We need to schedule an MRI immediately." The earliest Marilyn could have one done was the next day, Thursday, September 10, at 5:00 P.M.

Marilyn's neurologist was present while the MRI was in progress. The doctor said to me, "This appears to be the beginning of a stroke. Can you get Marilyn to Pittsburgh Presbyterian-University Hospital if I make the arrangements?" I told him that I could. The doctor asked us to return to our home and to wait for a phone call from Pittsburgh Presbyterian-University Hospital. We returned home and ate our supper together. It would be the last meal that Marilyn and I shared together in our home for more than ten weeks.

After supper I called my parents to tell them the news about Marilyn. My father was concerned about me and offered to drive us to Pittsburgh. I assured him that I was all right and was able to drive. At about 9:30 P.M., the admissions office from Pittsburgh Presbyterian-University Hospital called and told us to proceed to Pittsburgh. As we were driving to Pittsburgh, I experienced an inner peace and assurance even though the doctor said, "It looks like an acute stroke. I don't want to touch it with a ten-foot pole."

We arrived at Pittsburgh Presbyterian-University Hospital about 11:30 P.M. By the time Marilyn was admitted and taken to a room, it was about 1:00 A.M. Immediately a team of neurologists began to examine Marilyn. Needless to say, we did not get very much sleep that night. The next day, Friday September 11, the doctors determined by the EEG tests that were given to Marilyn that she was having frequent seizure activity. Immediately the doctors prescribed a seizure medication. Later that afternoon, the doctors prescribed an additional seizure medication because Marilyn was still seizing. At about 2:00 A.M. the next morning, Saturday September 12, a nurse came into Marilyn's room and said to us, "We are going to move you to the intensive care unit on 4F."

I asked, "Why? Is something wrong?"

As someone was pushing Marilyn's bed out into the hall, the nurse said, "Marilyn is still seizing, and she needs to be watched more closely. That can be done at the 4F intensive care unit."

When we arrived at the 4F intensive care unit, a nurse directed me to the 4F family waiting room. As I entered the waiting room, I saw two people trying to sleep. I later learned that they were a mother and her daughter. Immediately, the daughter said to me, "I'll find a blanket for you." As she gave me a blanket she asked, "Can I get you anything else?"

Immediately I said to myself, *The Good Shepherd is really looking out for me.* I thanked God for those people, and I remembered that special wedding anniversary gift that Marilyn gave to me.

None of us could sleep, so we started talking. It turned out that these people lived in the same community as Marilyn and I do. In fact, they lived on the same street as Marilyn did when she was living at home with her parents. These precious people knew Marilyn. Immediately I thought again, *The Good Shepherd is really looking out for Marilyn and me.* I told them all about Marilyn's situation. They then told me about theirs. A family member had a brain tumor and was recovering from surgery. I was thankful to our Lord for allowing me to meet those people. I knew that our meeting was not an accident or a coincidence. It was a divine appointment set by the Good Shepherd. Once again, I remembered that special twenty-fifth wedding anniversary gift that Marilyn gave to me.

I was able to see Marilyn about 10:00 A.M. that Saturday morning. She was not alert or awake. I spent about an hour with her and then decided to return to our home in Johnstown for the night. I wanted to return for several reasons. Sunday, September 13, 1998 was a special day in our church. We were having Sunday School Rally Day. Much work and prayer was given for this special day. Our Christian board of education set a goal of having 100 people in Sunday school that day. We planned to present awards to the class with the greatest percentage of their membership present and also to the child, youth, and adult who had the most guests with them in Sunday School that day. We planned to have a special Sunday School opening. We had scheduled a local puppet ministry team to have our Sunday School opening and then to also minister to the children in our Junior Church during the morning worship service.

I arrived home about 1:00 P.M. At approximately 4:00 P.M. that day, a doctor from Pittsburgh Presbyterian called and asked for my permission to put Marilyn on a ventilator. He said that the high dosage of seizure medication was affecting her breathing. I gave the doctor permission. At the time, September 12, 1998, I had no clue that Marilyn would slip into a coma that day and remain on the ventilator until Wednesday November 18th, 1998. (Marilyn had a tracheotomy on Monday October 5, 1998.) By the way, our Sunday School attendance was 88 on Sunday School Rally Day.

I had asked another minister and friend, Rev. Noah Martin, to preach that Sunday morning. I also asked him to lead our prayer time during the worship service. As Rev. Martin was praying during our prayer time, he called for me to come and kneel. He said to the congregation, "I sense God asking me to ask you to come and join with Pastor Guy in prayer. May we lay hands on him and ask for God's protection on Pastor Guy as he travels back and forth from

Pittsburgh, and may we ask for God's healing hand to be upon his wife, Marilyn."

As Rev. Martin and others prayed, the Holy Spirit reminded me again, "Jesus really is the Good Shepherd, and He also is the Great Physician." I knew that God's eye was upon me and that He had not forsaken me. That time of prayer was so very real and special to me. I was very grateful to my friend, Rev. Noah Martin, for being obedient to the Lord in asking others to join in prayer for me and with me.

As I traveled back to Pittsburgh that afternoon, I was glad that I was in church that morning. It was very difficult for me to be there, but I received so much love and encouragement from our church family. Our problems should not keep us from going to church. After all, what is the church all about anyway? It should be a place where we can find help and encouragement from God and one another. As I was driving, I could sense the love and presence of God all over me. That afternoon, there were several families that came to visit Marilyn and to offer me support and encouragement. Once again I realized that the Good Shepherd was watching over Marilyn and me. I remembered that special twenty-fifth wedding anniversary present from Marilyn.

Later that afternoon, I was made aware of the Family House. The Family House has rooms available at three locations for families of the hospital's patients. I called them and asked them to put my name on the waiting list for a room. On Tuesday September 15, a room became available at the Family House on McKee Place, just two blocks from the hospital. As I was checking in and receiving a tour of the building, I could sense the love and concern for me by the manager and those working at the Family House. Once again, the Holy Spirit brought to my attention, "Jesus really is the Good Shepherd, and He is watching over you."

Staying at the Family House was a real blessing to me. It gave me an opportunity to rest, study, and pray at my convenience. The Good Shepherd allowed me to meet several brothers and sisters in Christ during my stay there. The Good Shepherd also used me to minister to others during my stay there.

During our six-week stay in Pittsburgh, I think I witnessed about every possible human tragedy and emotion. But through it all, I was reminded over and over again that Jesus really is the Good Shepherd and that He can handle every hurt, every pain, and every seemingly impossible difficulty that we might face. "Is anything too hard for the Lord? At the appointed time I will return to you, according to the time of life, and Sarah shall have a son" (Gen. 18:14).

As I said before, time and time again God used other people and circumstances to remind me that Jesus was my Shepherd. Marilyn and I have a good neighbor and friend named Pete. Pete is a hunting and fishing buddy of mine and my father's. Pete and his wife, Nancy, along with Nancy's sister, Darla, have been attending my church for the last several years. Pete celebrated his eightieth birthday on September 6, 1998. Marilyn and I were blessed to eat lunch with Pete on his birthday at a local restaurant. Marilyn was anxious to give Pete a birthday gift that we had purchased at a local art-and-craft festival the day before. Marilyn noticed this item and said to me, "We just have to get this for Pete." It was a wooden plaque that had this saying on it: "Old fishermen never die, their bobbers just quit bouncing." We really had a good time together as Pete opened that gift. He knew that Marilyn had something to do with it.

One afternoon as my parents were preparing to leave Pittsburgh after visiting Marilyn, my father turned to me and said, "I almost forgot. Pete told me to shake your hand

and to tell you that the Lord is your Shepherd." When my father told me that, chills went up and down my spine. Once again, I remembered that special wedding anniversary gift from Marilyn. I thought to myself how good God is. God used a special friend of mine, who had just recently started to attend church—my church—to remind me that He certainly did not forget about me.

A few days later, Marilyn received a card that was signed by many people of our congregation. We have an encouragement table in the vestibule of our church. People in our congregation have the opportunity to sign cards that are sent to those of our church who are hospitalized or have reason to be encouraged by the church family. The encouragement table had been Marilyn's responsibility. Guess what the front cover of that special card said. It said: "The Lord is Your Shepherd."

A few days later, our district minister, Rev. Ronald Beachley, visited Marilyn in the intensive care unit. Guess what Rev. Beachley said to Marilyn as he was preparing to leave the room. That's right. He said, "Remember, Marilyn, the Lord is your Shepherd." Marilyn probably did not hear him say that, but I certainly heard it loud and clear. Some time later when Rev. Beachley visited Marilyn again, I told him how special that phrase was to me and how it encouraged me when he spoke those words to Marilyn a week or so before.

Over and over again, God kept reminding me through people and circumstances that Jesus was truly my Good Shepherd. He reminded me that not only was His eye on the sparrow but His eye was certainly on Marilyn and me.

I really need to ask this question to you as you read this Holy Spirit-inspired book: Have you allowed the Lord Jesus Christ to be your Shepherd? Have you invited the

Lord Jesus into your heart and life to be your Savior and Lord? Are you permitting the Lord Jesus to have control of every area of your life? Are you trusting in the Lord Jesus to be your Great Physician? The apostle Paul said, "For this reason I also suffer these things; nevertheless I am not ashamed, for I know whom I have believed and am persuaded that He is able to keep what I have committed to Him until that day" (2 Tim. 1:12).

Just as a safe can only keep and protect what we put in it, God will only keep and protect what we truly commit to Him. I strongly encourage you to fully commit every area of your life to the Lord Jesus. Just as most of us have rooms or closets in our homes that we would be embarrassed to let others see, don't have rooms or closets in your heart that would embarrass you if Jesus saw them. He really does see them anyway. Take the pressure off of yourself and let the Lord Jesus carry your difficulties, "Casting all your care upon Him, for He cares for you" (1 Pet. 5:8).

As I am writing this chapter, I am eating lasagna that the Good Shepherd provided for Marilyn and me through a member of our congregation. Thank You, Jesus, and thank you, Wendy. One Sunday a few weeks ago in church, Wendy gave the lasagna to me and said, "Put this in the freezer, and prepare it for you and Marilyn when she comes home."

I know that Wendy knows Jesus as her Good Shepherd. Wendy has two sons, Kevin and Keith, and she has been a single mom for the past several years now. Wendy has been very special to me for some time. I have watched Wendy trust in Jesus, her Good Shepherd, to meet every one of her needs. Wendy and her family live over thirty miles from the church, but she and her family are in church nearly every Sunday. In spite of all your problems, you can know Jesus as your Good Shepherd, too. He can handle any problem that you have.

2

The Diagnosis

Marilyn was in a coma for about ten days when the doctor said to me, "I think it's more than the medication that's keeping Marilyn in a coma. I think that there is something else going on. Can I have permission to do a spinal?" I gave him permission. Over the next few days, I gave the doctors permission to do various tests that would enable them to properly diagnose Marilyn's condition.

A few days later, a nurse gave me a copy of a case study of someone that had MELAS Syndrome. MELAS is the syndrome of mitochondrial encephalopathy, lactic acidosis, and stroke-like episodes. This disease is very, very rare. At the time of Marilyn's hospitalization in Pittsburgh, the doctors told me that there were only about one hundred fifty known cases of MELAS Syndrome in the world. The acronym MELAS was proposed for this syndrome in 1984. The condition of the woman described in the case study given to me described Marilyn's condition completely. In fact, as I was reading the case study, I thought that they were talking about Marilyn. There is no known cure for this syndrome. The person in the case study was treated with riboflavin and nicotinamide—precursors of coenzymes in the mitochondrial-electron transport chain. She had a slow but progressive return to previous functional status, and after nine months her symptoms had not returned. A nurse told me that it was a surprise to the doctors that this person returned to her previous functional status.

A few days later, one of Marilyn's doctors said to me, "We have a diagnosis. We believe that Marilyn has MELAS Syndrome. Over the weekend I will do some research to see if any new information is available to help us treat Marilyn."

My heart began to sink. My immediate thought was, *Only one hundred fifty people in the world, and Marilyn has to be one of them.*

As soon as I had that thought, the Holy Spirit spoke to me and said, "Don't you know that I know about Marilyn and the other approximately one hundred fifty people?"

I said, "Yes, Lord. I know that You know about them all. I know that You know about Marilyn. But why does Marilyn have to be one of these one hundred fifty people?" The Lord impressed upon me that He loves Marilyn more than I do or ever could. He created her and died for her.

Immediately the doctors began to treat Marilyn with the various vitamins and enzymes that were reported in that case study. One doctor said, "Let's give it some time and see what happens." One of Marilyn's neurologists told me that he personally knew of four other cases, none of which were in Pittsburgh. They were in Cleveland and Cincinnati where he had previously practiced. He later told me that two of those patients never came out of a coma.

The news of Marilyn's diagnosis spread rapidly. Many people expressed concern and assured me that they would be praying for Marilyn and me. Some had questions about Marilyn's diagnosis for which I had no answers. I heard that people were looking for information about the disease in health books, in libraries, and on the Internet. Some people had their human opinions about Marilyn's condition and wanted me to hear them. I knew that everyone meant well and just wanted to help in some way, but I really didn't want to hear everyone's opinion. The only opinion I wanted to hear was God's. At first I was asking myself, *Where are the people reminding me of what God's Word says about disease? Where are the people reminding me of what God has to say?* Perhaps some did not think that would have been necessary, since I was a pastor. However, everyone needs to be reminded of God's Word. Everyone, including pastors, needs to be encouraged by God's Word. "And let us consider one another in order to stir up love and good works, not forsaking the assembling of ourselves together, as is the manner of some, but exhorting one another, and so much the more as you see the Day approaching" (Heb. 10:24–25).

One thing I have learned over the years is that we always need to know, think, and speak God's Word and promises in spite of what our circumstances or symptoms are. God's Word says, "Death and life are in the power of the tongue" (Prov. 18:21).

From time to time, there were some who reminded me of a passage of Scripture pertaining to healing and God's presence with His children. Those reminders always came at the right times. My parents often had words of encouragement for me. Some members of my congregation reminded me of those passages in God's Word that pertain to healing. I was so thankful for Darryl and Tammy, the youth group leaders in our church. On just the second day of Marilyn's hospitalization in Pittsburgh, Darryl and Tammy came to Pittsburgh Presbyterian-University Hospital to encourage me.

I remember Marilyn's friend Becky saying to me, "This is not *the* valley."

Her husband, Ron, always said, "It's going to be all right. You'll see."

My friend Pastor Jack Rupert would call me some mornings while I was staying at the Family House. Jack always had a word of encouragement and a reminder from God's Word. Jack would always say to me, "Guy, I don't know what all is going to happen, but I do know that God is going to take care of you. Keep the faith." My friend Pastor Johnny Bryant of Lake Placid, Florida, also called frequently to be sure that I was "keeping the faith." Many people of his congregation sent words of encouragement and healing through the mail.

I'll always remember what these two special friends of mine said to me during the same week. One morning Pastor Jack telephoned me in Pittsburgh and said to me, "I had a dream about Marilyn last night."

Immediately I asked, "What was it about?"

Jack replied, "Oh, nothing special. We were just sitting around a table talking and laughing."

I remember saying to Jack, "This could be a word from God."

Jack answered, "Yes, it could."

Part of the Twenty-third Psalm reads, "You prepare a table before me in the presence of my enemies" (Psalm 23:5). God was certainly doing that for Marilyn and me.

Later that week my friend Pastor Johnny Bryant telephoned me and said almost exactly the same thing as Jack.

Johnny had had a dream about Marilyn as well. Marilyn was also laughing and talking in his dream. I said, " Johnny, someone else I know had the same dream. This could be from God."

Johnny answered, "It could very well be." In spite of what some believe, God does speak to His children through dreams and visions (see Joel 2:28, Acts 2:17). The dreams that my friends Pastor Jack and Pastor Johnny had were from God. I'll speak more about that in the last chapter, "The Rose Will Bloom Again."

God clearly spoke to me in dreams several times during my years of ministry. I would speak about them in this book, but the words from God were about personal needs of members of my congregation and pastor associates.

I know that there were many, many people praying and believing God for Marilyn's healing. One day during the weeks that Marilyn was in a coma, someone said to my friend Jack, "I sense God saying to me that Marilyn's sickness is not unto death." People that Marilyn and I had never met were praying for her.

Just this afternoon, January 15, 1999, as I was waiting for the elevator at Conemaugh Memorial Hospital, someone recognized me and asked, "How's your wife doing? Our prayer group has been praying for her for a very long time."

The Great Physician reminded me of His Word. "He was wounded for our transgressions, He was bruised for our iniquities; The chastisement for our peace was upon Him, And by His stripes we are healed" (Isa. 53:5).

During Marilyn's hospitalization in Pittsburgh, I became very defensive about Marilyn's condition. I only wanted positive news about her repeated. If I received negative news about Marilyn, I would only share that news with people who had great faith in God.

I tried to be as positive as I could around Marilyn's doctors and nurses. I kept saying to them, "She'll get there. She's in good hands." I was reminded of God's Word, "Whatever things are true, whatever things are just, whatever things are pure, whatever things are lovely, whatever things are of good report, if there is anything praiseworthy, meditate on these things" (Phil. 4:8).

I must say that it was very difficult for me to keep a positive outlook. The most difficult part of the day for me was the morning. It was very difficult for me to get out of bed and begin to face another day. I knew from God's Word that "God inhabits the praises of His people" (Ps. 22:3). It was difficult for me to give thanks and praise God. One evening as I was lying on my bed in my room at the Family House listening to the radio, my Good Shepherd, Jesus, led me to a local Christian radio station near Pittsburgh. That station played Southern gospel music in the mornings. Every morning when I awoke, I would reach for my walkman and listen to Southern gospel music. It was the Word of God in song that enabled me to keep a positive outlook concerning Marilyn's condition. Some days as I would walk from the McKee Family House to the hospital, I would have my walkman on and be listening to gospel music. Some days while eating breakfast in the hospital cafeteria, God would encourage me as I would listen to gospel music. The Holy Spirit reminded me of God's Word, "Therefore by Him let us continually offer the sacrifice of praise to God, that is, the fruit of our lips, giving thanks to His name" (Heb. 13:15–16). I learned to continually offer the sacrifices of praise. The Holy Spirit also reminded me of God's Word in Philippians 4:11–13, "Not that I speak in regard to need, for I have learned in whatever state I am, to be content: I know how to be abased, and I know how to abound. Everywhere and in all things I have learned both to be full and to be hungry, both to abound and to suffer need. I can do all things through Christ who strengthens me."

I learned to be content. I learned to offer the sacrifices of praise. Learning is neither optional nor an intellectual exercise for Christians. Christians learn because they are followers of Christ. The Lord Jesus Christ said, "Come to Me, all you who labor and are heavy laden, and I will give you rest. Take My yoke upon you and learn from Me, for I am gentle and lowly in heart, and you will find rest for your souls. For My yoke is easy and My burden is light" (Matt. 11:28–30). A part of love for God is expressed through learning which leads to faithful actions.

I wish that I was able to say that my attitude remained good during Marilyn's hospitalization. It did not. At times, I became frustrated and very impatient. I did not get angry with God, but I did become very impatient. I remember having a loud conversation with God in my bedroom one evening while I was in Johnstown. I was walking around in my bedroom, tossing my pillow around and saying to God very loudly, "I know Your Word is true! I know that many others are praying for Marilyn. I know that You are hearing these prayers. When will I see Your hand move on Marilyn's behalf? I need her, God." I would try to keep God's promises pertaining to healing fresh in my mind.

We all need to learn to apply God's Word to every situation in our lives. Most of our learning will not come in situations such as Sunday School and worship services. Most of our learning will occur in desperate, real-life situations. In the mid-'70s, I completed a four-year carpentry apprentice program. As I would read and study about things such as constructing concrete forms, wooden partitions, framing roof rafters, etc., I would say to myself, *I can do that.*

Anybody can do that. But it wasn't until I was out on the job site, working in the hot sun or the winter's cold with the boss watching every move I made, that I really began to learn. That's where we really learn about the love and power of God: out in the real world, in real-life situations.

The Holy Spirit reminded me that Jesus Christ is Lord. That word *lord* means "boss." The Holy Spirit reminded me of God's Word, "Therefore God also has highly exalted Him and given Him the name which is above every name, that at the name of Jesus every knee should bow, of those in Heaven, and those on earth, and of those under the earth, and that every tongue should confess that Jesus Christ is Lord, to the glory of God the Father" (Phil. 2:9–11). I believe that not only means every person, but also the name of every problem and every sickness and every disease.

I specifically remember one day as I was sitting beside Marilyn's side as she was in the intensive care unit at Pittsburgh Presbyterian-University Hospital. I took her by the hand and said, "MELAS, you must bow at the name of Jesus Christ. You must submit to the name and authority of Jesus Christ and His Word." At that moment, Marilyn did not get awake or move her body in any way. But I simply believed and quoted the Word of God.

At times, Marilyn's condition seemed to be improving. At other times, her condition seemed to be deteriorating. At times, Marilyn's body had much edema. At one point, she had as much as thirty-five to forty pounds of excess body fluid. People did not recognize her at times. Unless I was in the room and had told them it was Marilyn lying in the bed, they said they would not have known that it was Marilyn whom they were visiting.

I remember the day that a couple from our congregation, Matt and Lisa, came to Pittsburgh. Lisa had eye surgery that day, and her husband, Matt, came to visit Marilyn and me following the surgery. I visited them that night at their motel room in Pittsburgh. Matt said, "Rev, I would have never known that I saw Marilyn today had you not told me it was her. Lisa and I feel really bad. Everyone in the church feels really bad for you."

Even though the symptoms of our problems and circumstances remain following our application and belief of God's Word, we still must hold on to the Word of God. His promises are true and are available to all who believe in God and His Word.

As I am writing this chapter we are experiencing a winter storm here in western Pennsylvania. Our local meteorologists predicted this storm several days ago. When the weatherman predicts a storm like this one, don't even think about going to the grocery store. Fights break out in the parking lot over parking spaces. Fights break out in the store over grocery carts. Why? Everyone has to go get *their* bread and milk because the weatherman said that a storm was coming. I like our local weathermen, but sometimes they can't get yesterday's weather right. Why do we so easily believe a human being but be so slow in believing God's Word?

I specifically remember one day at lunchtime as I was exiting the hospital's cafeteria. One of Marilyn's doctors was standing in the hall, waiting for someone. I went to him and said, "How are you doing today, Doctor? Marilyn's doing good today."

He said to me, "You know, you're a very optimistic person. I'm a pessimistic person. I have to be in my profession. You're right. Marilyn is doing better today than I thought she ever would. She seems to be getting stronger every day."

I said to the doctor, "God's a good God." He just chuckled. Then I said, "You're a good doctor, too."

Remember, when your back is against the wall and you feel you're about to fall, you're just right for a miracle. So when you can't see it, expect it. When you can't feel it, expect it. A miracle you shall receive. All you have to do is believe. You're just right for a miracle. God still works miracles. "Jesus Christ is the same yesterday, today, and forever" (Heb. 13:8).

3

Bad Things Do Happen to God's People

One evening during my stay at the Family House on McKee Place, I met a very nice and interesting family in the basement lounge. Chris is an Asian produce farmer who lives in Costa Rica, Central America. He owns and operates a farm in Costa Rica and one in Homestead, Florida. I was curious as to why he and his family were there. Chris told me that he had had a benign tumor removed from his liver. For about fifteen minutes he described the whole process of how he came to Pittsburgh.

When Chris first began noticing pain and discomfort, he saw some doctors in Florida. He told me that they first thought that he had AIDS. Chris said, "No way. It is not possible." After some time and some convincing, Chris was diagnosed with the tumor on his liver. A doctor recommended that Chris have the operation at Pittsburgh Presbyterian-University Hospital. Chris then told me that he had had no hospitalization insurance. Chris was told that he needed to give the hospital $50,000 before they would perform the operation. Chris was able to do that, and then the operation was scheduled and performed. The operation was a success. Chris and his family were very grateful.

Chris then asked me what I did for a living and why I was there. I told him all about Marilyn's condition up until that day, and I then told him that I was a pastor. His eyes seemed to get bigger and brighter. He said, "My wife, Maria, and I went to Bible school in Costa Rica. Our church is very small—about thirty people. Two other guys and I lead our worship services and preach. We really do need a pastor." He continued, "You are a pastor, and your wife is very sick in the hospital? Bad things really do happen to Christians, don't they? I'm glad that we met because I know when I return home that some people will question why this happened to me when I am a Christian and do my best to live for God."

Chris and his family prayed for Marilyn every day. On the day that they returned to Florida, we all held hands and Chris prayed a very beautiful and special prayer for Marilyn. Chris' mother said to me, "Maybe a miracle will happen."

I said, "I sure hope so. God hears and answers prayer." God really used those people to encourage me. Once again, the Holy Spirit reminded me of that special twenty-fifth wedding anniversary gift that Marilyn gave to me. God certainly was being my Shepherd, and He had His eyes on Marilyn and me.

Yes, I have learned along with many others that bad things do happen to God's people. But what our enemy Satan means for harm God can turn into good. Shortly after our five-year-old daughter, Melissa, died on March 1, 1985, the Lord directed me to what has become a very meaningful verse of Scripture to me: "Blessed be the God and Father of our Lord Jesus Christ, the Father of mercies and God of all comfort, who comforts us in all our tribulations, that we may be able to comfort those who are in any trouble, with the comfort with which we ourselves are comforted by God" (2 Cor. 1:3–4).

I have learned that one of the reasons that seemingly bad things happen to Christians is so that we can experience the healing power and comfort of God and then allow God to use us to comfort and encourage others, just as His Word says to do. Also, God's Word says that "No temptation has overtaken you except such as is common to man; but God is faithful, who will not allow you to be tempted beyond what you are able, but with the temptation will also make the way of escape, that you may be able to bear it" (1 Cor. 10:13). That way of escape is the presence and the power of the Holy Spirit in our lives.

I'll never forget the phone call that I received at 1:00 A.M., March 3, 1993. When I answered the phone I heard these words, "Rev. Myers, someone in your congregation has had a tragedy. The family would like you to come to the hospital, if you can." My first thought was that someone must have been in an auto accident. However, I was told that a member of our church had just given birth to a child, a girl, but the baby was alive for only fifteen minutes and then died. The parents had prayed and planned for this child for a very long time. The delivery date had finally arrived and then this terrible tragedy had happened.

As I drove to the hospital, I was pondering what I could say to this family that could comfort them in any way at all. As I was pondering what to say, I heard the Holy Spirit speaking to me. He said, "Ask the mother and the family to look at you. You have been where they are now. Tell them that what God has done for you, He will do for them."

Had Marilyn and I not experienced the terrible loss of our daughter, I do not believe that I would have been able to minister to that family that night. That night, 2 Corinthians 1:3–4 became very real to me. That scripture had new meaning for me. I had experienced the comforting power of the Holy Spirit for eight years. I was now prepared to share with others what God had done for Marilyn and me.

All throughout the Bible we read of God's people experiencing difficult and trying times. But they allowed God to use those difficult times to advance the Kingdom of God. When we hear the names of most of the people in the Bible, we are reminded of their very difficult days. When we hear the name "Daniel," we are reminded of the time that he spent in the lions' den. When we hear the name "apostle Paul," we are quickly reminded of his days in prison and his trying missionary journeys. When we hear the name "Moses," we are reminded of the difficulty that many of God's people gave him as he was trying to lead them out of Egypt. When we hear the name "Noah," we are reminded of the ridicule that he must have endured as he labored for over 100 years constructing the ark that God told him to build. That ark was for the saving of Noah and his family. When we hear the name "David," we are quickly reminded of the time that he did battle with the giant, Goliath. I could mention many more names. These people all stand out and are easily remembered because of how they overcame their very difficult and trying circumstances. God enabled all of them to prevail in order to give all honor and praise to His Name.

God could have kept Daniel out of the lions' den, and He could have kept Paul and Silas out of prison. God also certainly could have kept the three Hebrew children out of the fiery furnace. But God never promised to keep us out of trying and difficult places. That's not the promise. He just promises to be with us.

In the New Testament, Peter writes, "In this you greatly rejoice, though now for a little while, if need be, you have been grieved by various trials, that the genuineness of your faith, being much more precious than gold that perishes, though it is tested by fire, may be found to praise, honor, and glory at the revelation of Jesus Christ, whom having not seen you love. Though now you do not see Him, yet believing, you rejoice with joy inexpressible and full of glory" (1 Pet. 1:6–8).

One song that we sing in our church at times is "Through It All."

> Through it all,
> Through it all,
> I've learned to trust in Jesus,
> I've learned to trust in God;
> Through it all,
> Through it all,
> I've learned to depend upon His Word.*

Wouldn't it be great if we lived in a perfect world? Unfortunately, we do not. We sing about being in the sweet "bye and bye" some day, but we're living in the nasty "now and now" today. There are days of doubt, days of unanswered questions, days of asking, "Why?" There are many days that cause us to want to throw in the towel and quit. But God commands us to persevere (see 2 Pet. 1:5–7).

The secret of perseverance is to never lose sight of where you are headed. "I press on that I may lay hold of that for which Christ Jesus has laid hold of me" (Phil. 3:12).

Yes, bad things do happen to God's people. Sometimes those bad times are sent by God.

* Text and Music by Andraé Crouch
  Copyright © 1971 by Manna Music, Inc., 35255 Brooten Road, Pacific City, OR 97135.
  All Rights Reserved
  Used by permission.

As I was making pastoral visits at a local hospital this afternoon, I saw another local pastor waiting for the elevator. He was having "one of those days." He asked me if I had had "one of those days" recently. I assured him that I did.

This pastor then shared a scripture with me, one that neither he nor I really noticed before: "For He commands and raises the stormy wind, Which lifts up the waves of the sea. They mount up to the heavens, They go down again to the depths; Their soul melts because of trouble. They reel to and fro, and stagger like a drunken man, And are at their wit's end" (Ps. 107:25–27 NKJV).

Were you ever at your wit's end? Maybe you feel as if you're at your wit's end today. If you are, I encourage you to notice Psalm 107:28–30: "Then they cry out to the Lord in their trouble, And He brings them out of their distresses. He calms the storm, so that its waves are still. Then they are glad because they are quiet; So He guides them to their desired haven."

God sometimes allows His people to pass through testing crucibles, trials of fire. James, the Lord's brother, has a word for us about that in James 1:2–4: "My brethren, count it all joy when you fall into various trials, knowing that the testing of your faith produces patience. But let patience have its perfect work, that you may be perfect and complete, lacking nothing."

The Lord is much more concerned about our willingness to be changed by Him into the image of His precious Son Jesus Christ than He is about our personal comfort. That's something that we in the modern church don't want to hear.

It was Mother Theresa who said, "You will never know that Jesus is all that you need until Jesus is all that you have." God wants us to learn and know that when everything else is stripped away from us, He is enough.

Yes, bad things do happen to God's people. But much good will come out of those "bad" times if we have faith in God and His Word. God will reveal Himself to us in those "bad" times if we only look for Him to do so. Perhaps you're going through a bad time in your life right now. If you are, I encourage you to look to God and His Word. Cry out to Him, because He will answer you. Surround yourself with people of great faith in God. If you do that, something good will happen to you.

4

Faith Comes by Hearing

"S o then faith comes by hearing and hearing by the Word of God" (Rom. 10:17). Marilyn wears hearing aids in both ears. She can hardly hear anything without them. After she had been in a coma for two weeks, one of her neurologists said to me, "I want you to put Marilyn's hearing aids in her ears. I think she will probably wake up soon." I could hardly wait to tell Marilyn's nurses what the doctor had just told me. They kept her hearing aids in a small plastic container on a shelf near Marilyn's bed.

When I finally was able to tell the nurses what the doctor said, they gave me the hearing aids. I then quickly realized that I had another problem. Marilyn's hearing aids are very small, and I realized that I did not have a clue as to which hearing aid went in which ear. I immediately asked the nurses if anyone could help me. Several nurses tried to come to the rescue, but none of them knew for sure which hearing aid went in which ear. Finally, one of the nurses and I thought that we had them in correctly. They seemed to fit.

The Good Shepherd then reminded me that those things take batteries. I needed to find Marilyn's hearing aid batteries the next time I returned to Johnstown. A few days later, I returned to our home in Johnstown and I found the hearing aid batteries. I knew that Marilyn kept some in her purse. The Good Shepherd also reminded me that Marilyn kept batteries in one of our kitchen cabinet drawers. As I was searching for those batteries, I found the owner's guide for the hearing aids. After looking through that information, I realized that her hearing aids were in the wrong ears. The left hearing aid has a telephone switch on it that enables Marilyn to hear better while talking on the phone. I knew that she put the telephone to her left ear.

God's Word says, "God's people perish for lack of knowledge" (Hos. 4:6). That is so very true. We perish spiritually and physically. If I had only paid more attention a long time ago to Marilyn's hearing aids, I wouldn't have made the mistake of putting them in the wrong ears. Their placement seemed right to me when I first put them in, but I was so very wrong. I really felt sorry for Marilyn for having a husband that knew so very little about her hearing aids simply because he had not paid better attention to them or to her.

I returned to Pittsburgh the next morning, and I could hardly wait to make sure Marilyn's hearing aids were working properly. I had batteries now. I wanted to be sure that she would be able to hear. When I was able to see Marilyn at the scheduled visiting time, I soon learned that I had another problem. As I was examining the hearing aids, I saw a substance around the volume control knob on one of the hearing aids. I asked one of the nurses for help in trying to remove this substance.

When I had most of it removed and had put a new battery in, I realized that the hearing aid was not working properly. Apparently it was damaged. Marilyn had had an MRI done the previous day. At that time, she had EEG leads attached to her head so she could be monitored for seizures. The EEG leads had to be removed, along with her hearing aids, when the MRI was done. A nurse apparently put Marilyn's hearing aids back in when she came back from the MRI. The person that reattached the EEG leads apparently did not know that Marilyn was wearing hearing aids. The substance used to hold the EEG leads accidentally got on the hearing aid and caused it to be damaged.

I called the company that Marilyn purchased the hearing aids from, South Hills Hearing Center. They told me to mail the damaged hearing aid to them and they would see if it could be repaired. Two days later, as I was preparing to leave my room at the Family House to visit Marilyn, the Lord impressed upon me to call the South Hills Hearing Center office. When the secretary answered the phone and realized it was me, she said, "You must have received my message."

I said, "What message?"

She said, "I just put a message on your answering machine asking you to call us."

I said, "I'm not in Johnstown. I'm staying in Pittsburgh for now as my wife is hospitalized at Pittsburgh Presbyterian." Once again, I was reminded that the Good Shepherd was certainly watching over Marilyn and me.

The secretary asked, "What in the world happened to that hearing aid?" I explained the whole thing to her. She said, "It will probably cost about $200 to repair it. If I were you, I would ask the hospital to pay the bill." I did that, and once again I realized that the Good Shepherd was watching over me.

About one week passed, and I felt impressed to call the hearing aid center to see if Marilyn's hearing aid was repaired. The secretary said, "You won't believe it. Someone just put your wife's hearing aid on my desk. We just got it back from the repair shop. I can put it in the mail today to your room in Pittsburgh, and you will probably receive it tomorrow."

I said, "Please give me directions to your office, and I will pick it up today." Their office building is about a thirty-minute drive from Pittsburgh Presbyterian-University Hospital.

Finally, Marilyn had both of her hearing aids working, and finally they were both in the right ears. From that day on, the very first thing I did every morning was to be sure Marilyn's hearing aids were in properly and working properly. I made sure that every nurse knew about them. I wanted to be sure that Marilyn was able to hear.

I need to ask you this question: Are you hearing properly? I'm referring to your spiritual ears. Is there anything blocking your spiritual ears from hearing the voice of the Good Shepherd? The Lord Jesus said, "My sheep hear My voice, I know them, and they follow Me" (John 10:27).

One evening as I was reading God's Word, the Lord directed me to Acts 14:8–10: "And in Lystra a certain man without strength in his feet was sitting, a cripple from his mother's womb, who had never walked. This man heard Paul speaking. Paul, observing intently and seeing that he had faith to be healed, said with a loud voice, 'Stand up straight on your feet!' And he leaped and walked."

God wants us to have faith in Him and in His Word. We have to be able to hear Him to have faith in Him. "Faith

comes by hearing, and hearing by the Word of God"
(Rom. 10:17).

Why Don't People Listen?
I believe that the most important communication skill
that anyone can have is to listen when someone is speaking
to them. One of the most frustrating things for me to deal
with were the many false statements that were being made
about Marilyn and her condition. It was almost unbelievable. What broke the camel's back was when someone told
me that it came across a prayer chain that I had to make a
decision on whether to pull the plug on Marilyn or not.
Nothing could have been further from the truth.
One day as I passed the information booth while entering one of our hospitals in Johnstown, someone asked me,
"What nursing home is Marilyn in?"
I said, "Nursing home? Marilyn's not in a nursing home.
She is a patient in this hospital." I remember making the
following comment to my congregation: "It wouldn't surprise me if I heard that Marilyn was on the space shuttle for
an experiment." (John Glenn was a passenger on the space
shuttle during that time.)
We are all guilty of not listening at times. Many of you
probably played the gossip game. Someone whispers a statement into someone else's ear. It then is repeated to others.
By the time it gets to the last person, the meaning of the
original statement is completely lost. I suppose that that
could be humorous at times, but I didn't find it very humorous at all.
The Lord Jesus said that some people around Him had
eyes but couldn't see and had ears but couldn't hear (see
Mark 8:18). Many times the Lord Jesus said, "And again I
say unto you . . ." I believe that He repeated Himself because He wanted to be sure that those to whom He was
speaking were really listening to Him. Are you listening

to the voice of God? Do you know when and what He is speaking to you?

A Bear Named Faith

Marilyn has a small collection of teddy bears. One day my sister Arla, her husband, Bernie, and son, Ryan, came to the hospital to visit Marilyn. Marilyn was not alert at that time. Arla, Bernie, and Ryan gave Marilyn a Ty teddy bear. It became very special to us for several reasons. First, this bear was kneeling and had praying hands. Nearly everyone who came to visit Marilyn commented on that bear. We knew that Marilyn was on nearly every prayer chain in Johnstown. We also were aware of family and friends across the country praying for Marilyn as well. This special Ty bear reminded me each and every day of the many people who were praying for Marilyn. I needed that reminder because sometimes I would forget that Marilyn and I were not in this valley alone. Many, many people were lifting us up before the Good Shepherd.

This Ty bear became very special for another reason. One day, about one week after this special gift was given to Marilyn, a nurse came into Marilyn's room and asked, "What is this bear's name?"

I said, "I don't know. I don't know if Marilyn named it yet."

The nurse said, "It already has a name." She opened the plastic, heart-shaped cover on the bear and said, "This bear's name is Faith." Wow! I later learned that my sister did not know about this special name either. Once again, I realized that the Good Shepherd was watching over Marilyn and me. My faith in the healing power of God began to increase. I know that Jesus is Lord. The Bible says, "Every knee shall bow and proclaim that Jesus is Lord" (Phil. 2:10–11). That means that the name of every sickness and disease must bow before the Lord Jesus Christ as well.

Once again I remember taking Marilyn's hand as she seemed to be sleeping, and saying, "MELAS Syndrome, you must bow at the name of Jesus. Jesus is Lord, not you, MELAS Syndrome. You must bow at the name of Jesus. By His stripes, Marilyn is healed." At that moment, Marilyn did not awake, she did not move, and I did not sense anything different within myself. I simply believed and recited God's Word.

"Then Jesus called a little child to Him, set him in the midst of them, and said, Assuredly, I say unto you, unless you are converted and become as little children, you will by no means enter the kingdom of Heaven" (see Matt. 18:2–3). All God wants us to do is simply believe and trust in His Word just as a child believes and trusts in his or her parents.

I knew that Marilyn had faith in God's Word. Throughout our twenty-five years of marriage, I saw her over and over again exercise her faith in God and His Word. In 1979, when our four-month-old daughter, Melissa, was diagnosed as having a "severe, developmental, delay, handicap problem," I saw Marilyn exercise her faith in God. Through Melissa's five-year life on earth, I witnessed Marilyn's faith in God increasing. On March 1, 1985, the day that God called Melissa back to Him, Marilyn's faith reached out to God. On July 1, 1985, Melissa's birthday, Marilyn had an emergency hysterectomy operation. Yet Marilyn's faith in God and His Word kept increasing. When God called me to full-time pastoral ministry, Marilyn had fears just like I did, yet her faith in God remained strong.

I remember one special afternoon that my parents visited Marilyn. When they entered Marilyn's room, Marilyn reached out to hug them. After a few minutes of conversation, Marilyn became silent. My mother said to Marilyn, "A penny for your thoughts?" Marilyn placed her hands in the position of praying hands. We knew that Marilyn was talking to her Lord.

When Marilyn finally returned home after her prolonged hospitalization, she seemed to have a difficult time sleeping at night. On the second night I said to her, "Do you want me to get one of those pills that were prescribed for you to help you sleep?" Marilyn replied, "No, I'm not getting hooked on those pills. Let's just ask the Lord to give me sleep." And so we did. Marilyn went to sleep very shortly after our prayer. Then I couldn't sleep because Marilyn was now snoring and I was also upset with myself because I, the preacher, was not the one to suggest to ask the Lord to give Marilyn sleep.

Over the years, I have preached many messages on faith. One truth that kept coming to me during this trying time was that God does not show partiality (see Acts 10:34). By that I mean that His promises that are given to us in His Word are for everyone. I kept remembering a passage of scripture in the book of James dealing with prayer and faith: "Confess your trespasses to one another, and pray for one another, that you may be healed. The effective, fervent prayer of a righteous man avails much. Elijah was a man with a nature like ours, and he prayed earnestly that it would not rain; and it did not rain on the land for three years and six months" (James 5:16–18).

Hebrews 11 is called the "Hall of Faith chapter." In this chapter, we read about heroes of faith. This passage identifies several characteristics of true faith.

1. Faith sees the invisible.
2. Faith hears the inaudible.
3. Faith believes the incredible.
4. Faith thinks the unthinkable.

5. Faith accomplishes the impossible
6. Faith inherits the indestructible.

FAITH HEARS THE INAUDIBLE

The greatest faith one can achieve is the ability to believe God when His voice is silent and His hand still. A victim of the German Holocaust scratched these words into the crumbling wall of his home before his death: "I believe in the sun, even when it does not shine. I believe in love, even when it is not shown. I believe in God, even when He does not speak."

I believe that most of the time the problem is not that God is not speaking. Rather, we are just not listening. Over the years I have learned some guidelines to recognizing the voice of God.

Guideline #1: We Must Have a Love Relationship with Jesus

The basic factor determining the communication of any two parties is the relationship between them. We were created for the supreme purpose of having a love relationship with Jesus Christ. Currently, the church of Jesus Christ is going through an engagement process with Jesus. One day the church will be married to Him. "That you may be married to another, even to Him who was raised from the dead, that we should bear fruit to God" (Rom. 7:4*b*). One day the church will attend the marriage supper of the Lamb (see Rev. 19:6–9)

I remember very well when Marilyn and I went through our engagement period. We never got tired of seeing one another or talking to one another. I remember returning home after one of our dates, and as soon as I got in the house I called her on the telephone. My father asked, "Who are you calling?"

I said, "I'm calling Marilyn."

He said, "Well, you just took her home." However, we wanted to talk and listen to each other more because we were very much in love.

That's the way it is with God's children now. We should be very much in love with Jesus. When we are, we will recognize His voice. I received several telephone calls this morning. Each time I did not have to ask who was calling. I recognized each voice immediately. Why? Because I had talked to each person many times before.

For us to move forward in God, we must be able to hear and to recognize the voice of God. Are you hearing from God? If not, examine your relationship with God. Perhaps it's not what it could be or should be. One of the most common statements I hear people make today is this: "I'm just so busy. I have so much to do."

The Lord Jesus said it would be that way. The Lord Jesus said, "And the cares of this world, the deceitfulness of riches, and the desires for other things entering in choke the word, and it becomes unfruitful" (Mark 4:19).

God says, "Hear, O My people, and I will admonish you! O Israel, if you would listen to Me! There shall be no foreign god among you; Nor shall you worship any foreign god. I am the Lord your God, Who brought you out of the land of Egypt; Open your mouth wide and I will fill it. But My people would not hear My voice, And Israel would have none of Me. So I gave them over to their own stubborn heart, to walk in their own counsels. Oh, that My people would listen to Me, that Israel would walk in My ways! I would soon subdue their enemies, and turn My hand against their adversaries" (Ps. 81:8–14).

Guideline #2: We Must Be Still to Listen to God

God's Word says, "Be still and know that I am God; I will be exalted among the nations, I will be exalted in the earth" (Ps. 46:10). That means that we must remove the inner noise as well as the outer noise. Most of us make life such a rush. We all have schedules to meet, problems to solve, and people to relate to. Did you ever try talking to more than one person at a time? It doesn't work very well, does it? We need to take the time to remove both the outer and inner noises so that we might hear God.

The Lord Jesus went to a lonely place to pray (see Mark 1:35, Luke 9:18).

Jesus also said that we should "Go into your room, and when you have shut the door, pray to your Father who is in the secret place; and your Father who sees in secret will reward you openly" (Matt. 6:6).

I wanted to hear from God concerning Marilyn's diagnosis. I wanted to know what God had to say about it. Many times it is very hard to tune out the inner and outer noises that surround us. That's why it is so very important to surround yourself with people that have great faith in God. Many evenings from my room in Pittsburgh, I would call my good friend Pastor Johnny Bryant, who pastors Lake Placid First Assembly of God in Lake Placid, Florida. He always helped me to tune out the inner and outer noises and to focus on the promises of God.

Another friend of mine, Pastor Jack Rupert, would call some mornings before I left my room at the Family House. God always had him call at the times that I was allowing inner noise to keep me from hearing from God.

One evening I called Rev. Russ Bixler and his wife, Norma. Rev. Bixler is an ordained minister in the Church of the Brethren. I had had him hold evangelistic services in my church on two occasions. He and his wife founded the Christian television station in Pittsburgh. Russ and Norma have great faith in God and have seen God heal many people. Rev. Bixler prayed a beautiful prayer of healing for Marilyn.

In Genesis 3:8 we read, "And they heard the sound of the Lord walking in the garden in the cool of the day." God wanted to talk to Adam and Eve. He also wants to talk to you and me. Do you know how to take a leisurely stroll with God and allow Him to speak to you?

Guideline #3: God's Voice Is Always Consistent with His Written Word

God will never say anything to you and me that contradicts His written Word. That's why it is so very important to have a basic working knowledge of His Word. If you want to know God's will, you must know His Word. Once we know His Word, we must speak His Word in spite of our present circumstances. "Death and life are in the power of the tongue" (Prov. 18:21).

Guideline #4: God's Voice Will Challenge Our Faith

"And when He had come into the house, the blind men came to Him. And Jesus said to them, 'Do you believe that I am able to do this?' They said to Him, 'Yes, Lord.' And He touched their eyes saying, 'According to your faith let it be to you'" (Matt. 9:28–29).

I have learned that many times God's voice does not make any human sense at all. God, however, just asks us to simply believe and obey. My good friend Pete gave me several gifts this past Christmas. One of those gifts was a poster that had the definition of faith printed on it. It said, "FAITH— Enables us to withstand what we can't understand."

Have you had your faith in God challenged lately? If not, perhaps you need to hear a fresh word from God. "For My thoughts are not your thoughts, Nor are your ways My ways, says the Lord. For as the heavens are higher than the earth, so are My ways higher than your ways, And My thoughts than your thoughts" (Isa. 55:8–9).

Faith does come by hearing, and hearing by the Word of God. There are about 9,000 radio signals in a metropolitan area, but without the aid of radio equipment the words and music go undetected. Likewise, faith is the faculty that enables us to sense God's direction.

Samuel was one of the mightiest prophets of the Old Testament. It is no coincidence that his first assignment from God necessitated that he learn how to hear God's voice. Read 1 Samuel 3:1–10. "Now the Lord came and stood and called as at other times, 'Samuel! Samuel!' And Samuel answered, 'Speak, for Your servant hears" (1 Sam. 3:10). Isn't that a beautiful way to answer God?

FAITH BELIEVES THE INCREDIBLE

God wants to do incredible things in your life. *Incredible* means "so extraordinary as to seem impossible or unbelievable." But you must first hear and then believe that God wants to do the impossible things in your life. Do you have some situations, problems, or circumstances that seem to be impossible to deal with or solve?

The Lord Jesus said, "If you can believe, all things are possible to him who believes" (Mark 9:23). The Lord Jesus said to two blind men who wanted to be healed, "Do you believe that I am able to do this?" (Matt. 9:28). Jesus then said to them, "According to your faith let it be to you."

On February 16, 1999, I was sitting with a family of my congregation in the waiting room of a hospital here in Johnstown. Bill was in the process of having heart surgery. When I first entered the waiting room, I noticed another family that seemed very distraught. Mark's wife, Nancy, had given birth to twins a few days earlier. But something became very wrong with her heart. Half of Nancy's heart was not functioning. She was put on a ventilator, and plans were being made to life-flight her to Pittsburgh Presbyterian-University Hospital.

I introduced myself to her husband, Mark. I then told him what God had just done for Marilyn. I remember looking at Mark and saying, "Mark, I do not know you, but God knows you. I know what God has done for my wife. He can do the same for your wife." Mark and I then asked the Great Physician to intervene and bring healing to Nancy.

I remember very clearly Mark saying to his very distraught family members, "Jesus is healing her right now. I know that He is. I know she will be all right."

"Death and life are in the power of the tongue" (Prov. 18:21).

I learned yesterday, March 3, 1999, that Nancy is now recuperating at home and is not expected to have any permanent heart damage.

Do you have any seemingly impossible situations in your life today? If you do, commit them to the Lord Jesus, the Great Physician. He can make a way where there seems to be no way. Hear God's Word. Believe God's Word. Then, believe and expect God to do His part.

God's Word states, "Now He [Jesus] did not do many mighty works there because of their unbelief" (Matt. 13:58). Imagine, people in Jesus' hometown not expecting or believing that the Lord Jesus would do the impossible!

Faith does come by hearing, and hearing by the Word of God. I remember when I was first learning to recognize, hear, and believe God's voice in my life. It was during the very beginning years of my pastoral ministry. I remember wrestling with the decision to begin the local pastors' training school, then wrestling with the decision to begin Bible college. I remember wrestling with the decision to begin my first part-time pastorate. I was asked to be the part-time pastor of a very small congregation which was located forty miles from our residence. I am so glad that I recognized and responded positively to God's voice and call. Marilyn and I have many fond memories of those days of ministry from 1983–1985. We still hear from people of that small congregation.

I remember wrestling with the decision to accept my first full-time pastorate. My mind was saying, *Don't accept it. Are you crazy?*

However, I heard God saying, "This is where I want you to serve now." That was ten years ago. I am so glad that I heard, believed, and responded positively to God's Word.

The Lord Jesus asked doubters and skeptics to stay away from Him one day as He was about to bring a dead girl back to life (see Mark 4:35–43). We, too, need to choose very wisely the people that we have close fellowship with. We all need spiritual mentors.

Don't keep the power of God away from your family, ministry, church, or any of life's problems and challenges because of a lack of faith or unbelief. "Now to Him who is able to do exceedingly above all that we ask or think, according to the power that works in us" (Eph. 3:20).

5

Ministering to Others
while Waiting on God

I remember preaching to my congregation and saying, "When you have major problems, ask the Lord to help you focus on someone else's need and allow God to use you to help them. That will greatly help you in dealing with you own difficulty."

Marilyn was admitted to Pittsburgh Presbyterian-University Hospital on September 10, 1998. I was scheduled to conduct evangelistic services for two local congregations: The Maple Grove Church of the Brethren services were scheduled for September 27–30, 1998, and the Tire Hill Church of the Brethren services were scheduled for October 11–14, 1998. I really enjoy holding evangelistic services and watching God move among His people. I am good friends with both of the current pastors of these congregations. Pastor Mike Christine and Pastor Jack Rupert were a great help to me throughout Marilyn's hospitalization. I wanted to keep these two speaking appointments, and yet I didn't. I wanted to go out and minister, but yet I wanted to be by Marilyn's bedside as much as I could. I also was saying to myself, *Marilyn and I need to be ministered to right now. Surely God understands that.* I did not speak at the scheduled Maple Grove services. Pastor Christine was successful in securing other local pastors to speak.

Marilyn had been a patient at Pittsburgh Presbyterian-University Hospital for about two weeks when I received a phone call from another pastor in Johnstown. He told me that a faithful member of his congregation was life-flighted to Pittsburgh Presbyterian-University Hospital the night before. She apparently had heart problems. This pastor asked me if I would visit with her and her family. I must confess to you that my very first thought was not what it should have been. I said to myself, *My wife is in the intensive care unit, in a coma, on a breathing machine, and this guy is asking me to visit one of his members? Why doesn't he drive to Pittsburgh and visit his own people?*

As soon as that thought rushed through my mind, the Holy Spirit convicted me. "Don't you know and remember that you have committed Marilyn to Me? Don't you think that I can watch over her while you visit with this person in need for a few minutes? Don't you think that pastor would go to Pittsburgh now if he could? This is your mission field while you are here. Minister! I will enable you." I was really convicted, and I repented.

The very next day, I visited with Vera and her family. I was so glad that I did. Vera and her husband really love the Lord and serve Him faithfully in their local church. Vera had some blockage in some arteries around her heart. The blockage was able to be removed by the angioplasty procedure. Vera and her family assured me that they would pray for Marilyn. Later, when Marilyn was transferred back to

Johnstown and doing much better, Vera's husband, Harry, visited Marilyn. That was a special day.

The following week I received another telephone call from the same pastor. Another member of his congregation was having surgery the next day to have a tumor that was located near her brain removed. I didn't think any bad thoughts this time. I assured him that I would visit this young woman. When I did, I recognized both her and her husband. This woman's husband was severely burned on the job a year earlier. I had traveled to Pittsburgh at that time with this same pastor to visit with him and another mutual acquaintance that was fighting leukemia. We had a special time of prayer together in this woman's room. Her surgery went very well. Her hospital stay was short. She was able to attend church the following Sunday.

A few days later, I received word that a relative of one of my church members was hospitalized in Pittsburgh Presbyterian-University Hospital. He had just had surgery and was not doing very well at that time. It was a real joy to visit with him and his family. They also expressed concern for Marilyn, and God used them to encourage me.

A few more days went by, and I learned that Dan's nephew, John, was hospitalized in Montefiore Hospital. (Dan is a member of our congregation. His nephew, John, has some type of blood disorder.) John seemed to have a very positive attitude, and God used him to encourage me.

During our six-week stay in Pittsburgh, I had plenty of opportunities to minister to others. I'll never forget Linda. I was waiting in the 4F waiting room for the next scheduled visiting time when my attention was drawn to Linda and those standing around her. The first words I heard her say were, "Do you know what [so and so] said to me when I got here? He said, 'Remember, Jesus loves you.' I wanted to hit him."

I immediately thought to myself, *Here is a ministry opportunity.* I learned the next day that it was Linda's fiancé who was just admitted. He was a United Methodist pastor who had just resigned his pastorate a few weeks prior. He needed surgery for an aneurysm, and he was not in very good condition.

Linda and I had many interesting conversations during the time that Marilyn was in the 4F intensive care unit. We were able to laugh and cry together. She also began to really let Jesus, the Good Shepherd, carry her through this very difficult time in her life.

I'll never forget a very nice lady that stayed at the Family House for about one week. Her name is Georgie. Georgie's husband was a patient at Pittsburgh Presbyterian-University Hospital. He was dying from cancer. When I first met Georgie, she said to me, "What I like about this place is that everyone helps each other." She told me all about her husband's illness. He had been fighting cancer for a long time. I told her that I would remember him in my prayers. At that time, he was in the same intermediate care unit that Marilyn was in. Georgie then asked why I was there. I told her all about Marilyn's condition. She assured me that she would put Marilyn on her church's prayer chain.

A day or two later I noticed Georgie in the hospital's cafeteria eating supper by herself. The Lord directed me to sit with her. Marilyn did not have a good day that day, and God really used Georgie to minister to me. During our conversation we talked about the physical exercise that we were getting walking back and forth between our rooms at the Family House to the hospital. (The hospital was built on a steep hillside.) The name "Cardiac Hill" kept coming up in our conversation. Georgie then said to me, "Do you know that you can avoid Cardiac Hill? There is an underground walkway that has an exit on Fifth Avenue."

I said, "I didn't know that, and I've been here for three weeks."

Georgie said, "When we are finished eating, I'll show you the way." A few minutes later God used Georgie to show me how to avoid that dreaded Cardiac Hill. Before we separated, Georgie said again, "We have to help each other out. You helped me, and now I helped you. That's what I like about this place: Everyone helps each other."

If you are a Christian, God wants to use you to help others and to show them the way. "And the things that you have heard from me among many witnesses, commit these to faithful men who will be able to teach others also" (2 Tim. 2:2).

One day in the hospital cafeteria, the Lord arranged for me to meet Tom. When I first saw Tom, he smiled at me as if he knew who I was. I sat next to him as I was eating my lunch. Tom's wife was a patient at the Montefiore Hospital. She had had major surgery done in her mouth because of cancer. Her tongue was removed and her jawbone had been reconstructed. Tom began to share with me some of his frustrations. His wife was practically deaf. She couldn't talk. She had a very difficult time eating because her tongue was removed. Because his wife was practically deaf, sometimes communicating with the doctors became very difficult.

I expressed to Tom how I was experiencing that same frustration. Sometimes Marilyn's hearing aids would not be properly placed in her ears when the doctors came to see her in the morning. The nurses would remove a hearing aid to take Marilyn's temperature. Many times the hearing aid was not put back in her ear properly. Other times the volume control was moved during the night. So sometimes Marilyn just couldn't hear or understand the doctors as they were trying to communicate with her. Marilyn was unable to express to them at those times that she wasn't hearing them.

I know that the Good Shepherd brought Tom and me together so that we might be able to encourage and comfort one another. During the remainder of our stay in Pittsburgh, Tom and I made arrangements to meet for lunch or supper. We exchanged telephone numbers and addresses before leaving Pittsburgh. We have talked several times since our wives were discharged and we returned to our homes.

Taking the time to minister to others during our six-week stay in Pittsburgh helped me as much as it did anyone else. God gave me the strength to do it and the words to say to others. I also realize now that during those ministry times Satan did not have as much opportunity to plant negative thoughts in my mind. My mind was occupied with trying to hear from God. God's Word says, "Now if we are afflicted, it is for your consolation and salvation, which is effective for enduring the same sufferings which we also suffer. Or if we are comforted, it is for your consolation and salvation. And our hope for you is steadfast, because we know that as you are partakers of the sufferings, so also you will partake of the consolation" (2 Cor. 1:6–7).

God always knows what we need, and He always brings the people into our lives that He can use to help meet those needs. One of Marilyn's and my favorite Scripture verses is Hebrews 13:2, "Do not forget to entertain strangers, for by so doing some have unwittingly entertained angels."

This afternoon I was talking to Wendy on the telephone. Wendy wrecked her car yesterday during the winter storm that hit our area. She told me all about the accident and also about her youngest son, Keith, who was ill and had a temperature. Even though Wendy had these extra needs, she was telling me how God was using her to minister to a friend of hers who recently separated from her husband.

In spite of what you might be going through today, look for ways that God can use you to minister to others. It will help you as much as it will help the person that you minister to. Allow God to use you to minister to others while you wait upon God to meet your needs.

The Word of God tells us about a widow who lived in Zarephath. There was a great famine in the land of Zarephath at that time. The prophet Elijah saw this widow at the gate of the city, and he asked her to give him a drink of water and a morsel of bread (see 1 Kings 17:10–11). She answered Elijah and said, "As the Lord your God lives, I do not have bread, only a handful of flour in a bin, and a little oil in a jar; and see, I am gathering a couple of sticks that I may go in and prepare it for myself and my son, that we may eat it, and die" (I Kings 17:12).

And Elijah said to her, "Do not fear; go and do as you have said, but make me a small cake from it first, and bring it to me; and afterward make some for yourself and your son. For thus says the Lord God of Israel: 'The bin of flour shall not be used up, nor shall the jar of oil run dry, until the day the Lord sends rain on the earth.'" The widow did as Elijah said, and she and her son ate for many days.

Later, the widow's son became sick and died. Elijah carried him to the upper room where he was staying and laid him on his own bed. Elijah stretched himself out on the child three times and prayed that God would restore life back to his body. God answered Elijah's prayer. As Elijah handed the son back to his mother she said, "Now by this I know that you are a man of God, and the word of the Lord in your mouth is the truth" (1 Kings 17:24).

While she was in great need herself, God used this widow to minister to someone else. Through it all God was with the widow and met every one of her needs. He will do the same for you and me. How do I know? "Jesus Christ is the same yesterday, today, and forever" (Heb. 13:8). Praise His name!

Our Lord did enable me to hold the evangelistic services at the Tire Hill Church of the Brethren October 11–14, 1998. I was so glad that I was able to hold those services. The people of the congregation really encouraged me during those days, and God also moved during the services. People came to the altar every night for prayer and healing. My burden became lighter as I allowed God to use me to minister to others as I was waiting on Him for Marilyn's healing.

I drove back and forth from Pittsburgh to Johnstown during those days. That gave me an opportunity to spend time with family and friends. One of those days, my father drove me to see Marilyn. Marilyn was very alert that day. Before we had to leave, Marilyn said, "Let's pray." That was a special time of prayer. Another day, Marilyn's friend Becky traveled with me to see Marilyn. She was anxious to see Marilyn because I told her how alert Marilyn had been the day before.

6

The Day after the Prayer Vigil

I returned to Johnstown early Saturday morning October 3, 1998. I needed to do laundry, pay some bills, and finish preparing for the Sunday morning worship service. I was somewhat nervous and apprehensive that particular weekend because Marilyn was scheduled to have a tracheotomy done on Monday, October 5. Marilyn had been on the ventilator for three weeks now. The doctors really wanted to do the tracheotomy about a week earlier, but I wanted them to wait as long as they possibly could. I kept praying that Marilyn would be able to come off the ventilator and not need the tracheotomy.

Another reason that I was hesitating in letting the doctors do the tracheotomy on Marilyn was that I thought she would be very upset about it later. I was not sure of how aware she was of her condition. The last thing that I wanted to do was to upset her more.

When I arrived at the church early that Sunday morning, October 4, I noticed in the bulletin that the church had scheduled an all-day prayer vigil for Marilyn on Wednesday October 7. I began to weep as soon as I read that. Our congregation has the good reputation of being a praying church. Marilyn and I certainly needed people praying for us.

That Sunday morning worship service was very meaningful to me. We had a local gospel quartet, Four for One, for special music. They are really good. I also sensed a special anointing on the morning message. As I traveled back to Pittsburgh that afternoon, I really had a peace in my heart. I sensed God speaking to me saying, "Don't fear. I am with Marilyn, and I am with you."

As scheduled, Marilyn had the tracheotomy done the next day, October 5, 1998. I'll probably never forget seeing her right after the tracheotomy was done. Marilyn looked a little more like herself. My first thought was, *Perhaps I should have permitted the tracheotomy to be done sooner.* There wasn't much change in Marilyn from Monday October 5 through Wednesday October 7.

But remember, our congregation was praying on Wednesday, October 7.

I returned to Johnstown on Wednesday evening to take care of some responsibilities at home and at the church. The next morning in my study at the church, the telephone rang. It was one of our deacon couples, Don and Pat Garman calling. They asked if I thought it would be good for them to visit Marilyn that day in Pittsburgh. I told them I thought it would be good, and we made plans to meet for lunch along the way.

When we arrived at Marilyn's bedside, I could hardly believe what we were seeing. Marilyn was sitting up and seemed to be awake and alert. She began to ask me questions such as, "What floor am I on? . . . When did this happen? . . . What's the weather like outside?"

When the nurse passed nearby, Marilyn asked to have a drink of water. The nurse told her no and also why she couldn't give her a glass of water. The nurse said, "How about if I wet your lips and mouth with a wet swab?" Marilyn just rolled her eyes.

About that time, two of Marilyn's neurologists came by. Marilyn asked one of them for a drink of water. He told her the same thing as the nurse had. The doctor then said, "How about an ice chip?" Marilyn agreed, and the nurse gave her one. A few minutes later, the nurse was suctioning some fluid around Marilyn's trachea.

She then said to Marilyn, "Do you have anything in your mouth?"

Marilyn answered, "Yeah, my tongue." She then stuck her tongue out at the nurse.

While one of the doctors was examining Marilyn, the other doctor noticed that she was following her nurse with her eyes. The doctor became very excited and said to me, "I might have given you a wrong prognosis about Marilyn."

I put my arm on his shoulder and said, "God's a good God, doctor. Remember, we said before that only God knows what will become of Marilyn."

I believe that the day of our church's planned prayer vigil was the beginning of Marilyn's miraculous touch from the Great Physician. She did have many bad days after that, but I really believe the seed of faith was beginning to blossom. Marilyn communicated so much that day following the prayer vigil. Don's mother, Gertrude, was hospitalized in Johnstown at this time. Marilyn liked to talk to Gertrude, and we told Marilyn about Gertrude's hospitalization. Marilyn expressed concern and asked what was wrong.

I kept repeating over and over, "I can't believe it! I can't believe how much Marilyn is communicating today." Don reminded me that the church was praying the day before.

Seeing a big change in Marilyn on the day following our church's prayer vigil reminded me of the time in Jesus' ministry when He healed a paralytic man. This is recorded in the second chapter of the Gospel of Mark. As Jesus was ministering in Capernaum, many people gathered around to hear Him. The Bible states, "Immediately many gathered together, so that there was no longer room to receive them, not even near the door" (Mark 2:2).

There were four men carrying a paralytic man trying to see Jesus. They wanted Jesus to touch and heal this man who was paralyzed. The Bible states, "And when they could not come near Him because of the crowd, they uncovered the roof where Jesus was. So when they had broken through, they let down the bed on which the paralytic was lying" (Mark 2:4).

The crowd, the "because," did not stop these four men from doing what they could to see Jesus. There will always be "becauses" in our life. Some people might have said, "It must not be God's will for Jesus to heal this man today *because* of the crowd. If it was God's will, the crowd would not be there." I can just hear some people making that comment. During my years of ministry I've heard many becauses, or excuses. Some of them were "Because I'm too busy. . . . Because I'm too tired. . . . Because I've tried it before. . . . Because it's too difficult."

The crowd, or the "because," did not stop these four men from taking their friend to Jesus. The Bible states,

"When Jesus saw their faith, He said to the paralytic man, 'Son, your sins are forgiven you'" (Mark 2:5).

After some of the scribes accused Jesus of blasphemy, Jesus said, "'But that you may know that the Son of Man has power on earth to forgive sins,'—He said to the paralytic, 'I say to you, arise, take up your bed, and go to your house.' Immediately he arose, and went out in the presence of them all, so that all were amazed and glorified God saying, 'We never saw anything like this'" (Mark 2:10–12).

I am learning that all great spiritual victories lie on the other side of the "becauses." Even Jesus became tired and weary, but He did not allow that to stop Him from ministering to the woman at the well (John 4:1–29).

The "becauses" in our lives should stimulate our faith and encourage us to unite with others and take our impossibilities to Jesus. Nothing happens until we meet Jesus. I will always be eternally grateful to the many individuals and local church prayer teams that were praying for Marilyn. From time to time someone would say, "Remember, you're not alone. Many are praying for Marilyn and you." I really needed to be reminded of that fact, because at times it did seem that I was all alone. But thanks be to God that many people in Johnstown and across the nation were united in prayer for Marilyn.

I'm reminded of the time that Peter was in prison. "So when he had arrested him, he put him in prison, and delivered him to four squads of soldiers to keep him, intending to bring him before the people after Passover. Peter was therefore kept in prison, but constant prayer was offered to God for him by the church" (Acts 12:4–5). I knew my congregation and many other local congregations were praying for Marilyn and me, and I was thankful. One reason it's so important for you to be a part of a local church that believes in the power of prayer is that when trouble comes your way, you will not be alone. Others will be able and willing to pray with and for you. It will be a great comfort to you as it was to me.

As I mentioned earlier, Marilyn also did have many bad days in Pittsburgh after our church's prayer vigil. Some of her problems included developing pancreatitis on several occasions, and she had very high temperatures from time to time. She also needed to receive four units of blood; she twice received two units in about a ten-day period. I remember one day Marilyn's nurse said to me that they were going to move her IV connection from her groin area to an area on her shoulder. Shortly after it was relocated the nurse said, "It's possible that Marilyn was losing blood from that location." We couldn't understand why she needed to have those four units of blood in a short amount of time.

I went to visit Marilyn one day after returning from Johnstown. She was in the intermediate care section at that time. When I entered the intermediate care area I noticed that Marilyn was not there. I immediately asked for her nurse. The nurse said, "We moved Marilyn to the intensive care unit across the hall."

"Why?" I asked.

The nurse replied, "We noticed that Marilyn had a very weak pulse in her right foot. Her foot also was very cold. She can be watched more closely in the intensive care unit." Throughout this time Marilyn had a lot of edema and her blood pressure remained high and unstable. The doctors were debating whether to have Marilyn's feeding tube surgically placed in her stomach.

The Holy Spirit reminded me of Jonah in the Old Testament. Jonah called his symptoms "lying vanities" (Jon. 2:8). In spite of Jonah's surroundings as he was in the belly of that great fish, he said, "But I will sacrifice to You with the voice of thanksgiving; I will pay what I have vowed. Salvation is of the Lord" (Jon. 2:9).

From time to time as I would consult with Marilyn's doctors, they reminded me that neurologically Marilyn was fine. Her major problems were now medical ones. Throughout this very stressful and difficult time, I knew that Marilyn's doctors and nurses were doing their part. I also knew that very many people were praying for Marilyn. I remember talking to my friend Rev. Noah Martin one evening on the telephone. After I gave him a report of Marilyn's condition, I'll never forget Rev. Martin saying to me, "God certainly has to do something very soon. I think all of Johnstown is praying for Marilyn." We both knew that God already was ministering and responding to prayer, but He was about to manifest Himself in a very special way.

7

Going Back to Johnstown

Marilyn had been hospitalized in Pittsburgh Pres-byterian-University Hospital for about four weeks when her doctors told me that I should begin searching for another facility to admit Marilyn for therapy and rehabilitation. They encouraged me to contact a social worker for advice. I didn't realize it at the time, but a social worker was already assigned to me.

During my first meeting with the social worker, she asked me several questions pertaining to Marilyn's ability to obey and follow commands. Marilyn really was not do-ing much at all at that point in time, but I did notice her moving her arms and legs at times. At least she would move her legs when I would tickle the bottoms of her feet.

The social worker said that it would be Marilyn's ability to listen and obey orders which would largely determine what facility would consider accepting her. She mentioned several facilities closer to our home in Johnstown that were possibilities.

A few days after my first meeting with the social worker, I was made aware of a new skilled nursing facility that had just opened the first week of October 1998. After visiting this facility and meeting some of the administrative people and nurses, I gave this information to my social worker at Pittsburgh Presbyterian-University Hospital. I was later told that this new skilled nursing facility in Johnstown had accepted Marilyn as a patient. Arrangements were now beginning to be made to transfer her to this new facility. Marilyn would be transferred as soon as her doctors at Pittsburgh Presbyterian Hospital agreed that Marilyn was stable and physically able to make the trip.

On October 17, 1998, I was told that Marilyn would be transferred to Johnstown on Monday October 19, 1998. I was so excited. Finally, we would be able to leave Pittsburgh and go back to our hometown. I remember thinking, *Finally, I'll be able to sleep in my own bed again.*

Well, Marilyn developed a temperature the next day. I remember one of the nurses saying to me, "Marilyn probably will not be transferred until Tuesday now. The doctors will want to monitor her temperature."

The next few days were very stressful. For one reason or another, Marilyn was unable to be transferred. It seemed that something was always going wrong with her physical condition. If she didn't have a temperature, she needed blood for some reason. If she didn't need blood, she developed an infection somewhere in her body. If it wasn't an infection, her blood pressure was out of control again. Something was always going wrong and delaying the transfer back to Johnstown.

Finally, I was told on Thursday afternoon October 22, 1998 that Marilyn would be transferred to Johnstown the next day. The arrangements had all been made. Marilyn was scheduled to leave Pittsburgh Presbyterian-University Hospital at 11:00 A.M., October 23, 1998. Everyone was very excited. We were hoping and praying that there would not be any unexpected setbacks with her physical condition so that she could make the trip to Johnstown.

I was at Marilyn's bedside at 9:00 A.M. on Friday October 23, 1998 waiting for confirmation from the doctor that she was going to Johnstown that day. When the doctor finally arrived, he was somewhat reluctant to transfer Marilyn that day. I remember very well the doctor saying to me, "This is not an ordinary transfer. Your wife is somewhat unstable." He was concerned about Marilyn's digestive system. Finally, after consulting another doctor, he said, "The ambulance will be here at 11:30 A.M. to transfer Marilyn to Johnstown."

I immediately went back to Marilyn's bedside and told her the good news. Even though Marilyn was looking at me as I was speaking to her, I wasn't sure that she was comprehending what I was telling her. I told her I visited this new facility, the people seemed very nice and friendly, and that the entire environment seemed good. I also told her that there were two beds in her room and that I would be able to stay overnight if she wanted me to.

Finally, the ambulance arrived and we were on our way back to Johnstown, Pennsylvania. I traveled in my own vehicle and went immediately to our house to take care of some business. I also wanted to give Marilyn time to get settled in her new room.

When I went to Marilyn's bedside later that afternoon, it was very obvious that the trip home was very tiring for her. She would open her eyes occasionally when I called her name. At one point I said to her, "Marilyn, you're back in Johnstown." She nodded her head in the affirmative. Marilyn had received approximately 125 get-well cards while hospitalized in Pittsburgh. While she rested, I taped them all to the wall facing her. I then returned home early that evening as Marilyn seemed to be in a deep sleep.

When I returned to her bedside the following morning, Marilyn's eyes were wide open, and I could read her lips as she said, "I thought you were going to stay here overnight." I felt a sense of relief knowing that Marilyn seemed to be aware of where she was.

The next day, Sunday October 25, 1998, was my birthday. I didn't know if I should tell Marilyn it was my birthday or not. I knew that she did not have a clue as to how long she had been hospitalized. When I entered her room that day it was about 2:00 P.M. I had led our morning worship service and also had lunch with my parents. When Marilyn saw me entering her room she said, "It's about time."

I know that I had a smile on my face because I remember having the thought, *I have my wife back. She's scolding me, and I don't mind at all.* I told her why I did not arrive until 2:00 P.M. I then said, "Marilyn, today is my birthday."

She looked at me and said, "I'm sorry. I didn't get you anything." I assured her that I didn't mind. Marilyn has always been very mindful of the birthdays and anniversaries of our family and friends. She always was sure to have a gift to give on those occasions.

Marilyn was alert that afternoon and was aware that I would be at our 7:00 P.M. church service that evening. Before I departed that afternoon, Marilyn said to me, "Will you stop back after church?" I told her that I would.

When I arrived back to her room after the service, I received an unpleasant surprise. Marilyn was in respiratory distress. She had approximately thirty pounds of excess body fluid at that time. As her local neurologist was exiting her room shaking his head, he said to me, "This is really some disease." I immediately telephoned my parents and asked them to place Marilyn on our church's prayer chain. I stayed with Marilyn for about two hours. It was very difficult watching her trying to breathe. Her nurse assured me that it was all right for me to go home to try to get some rest. Marilyn's condition did not improve much at all the remainder of that week. In fact, I believe that it got worse.

Except for Sunday, October 25, she did not communicate or respond much at all that week.

The Cardiac Arrest

On October 31, 1998, at about 9:30 A.M., I received a telephone call from someone at the Conemaugh Valley Memorial Hospital. A woman said to me, "Mr. Myers, your wife, Marilyn, is in cardiac arrest. She will be transferred to the intensive care unit here at the hospital." She then added, "I'm not sure how long her heart was stopped, but they did bring her back."

After I made a few telephone calls, I went immediately to the intensive care unit. Marilyn had not yet arrived. She was still at the other facility, which was just right up the street from the hospital. Our district minister, Rev. Ron Beachley, arrived at Marilyn's room about the same time. Marilyn's doctor was also there. He said to me, "We're not sure what happened. We sat Marilyn up in bed so that we could take an x-ray, and her heart stopped. She was brought back immediately. Hopefully everything will turn out." Shortly after that, Marilyn was taken to the hospital's intensive care unit. There is a covered walkway that is connected to the hospital and to the building where Marilyn was. Rev. Beachley and I were able to walk beside Marilyn's cart as she was taken to the intensive care unit.

That evening my friend Rev. Noah Martin visited with me in my home. He had been keeping abreast of Marilyn's condition since her hospitalization. He was very concerned

83

about Marilyn and me. Rev. Martin and I had some heart-to-heart conversation that night. I'll always remember the prayer time that we shared together as we were on our knees in my living room.

Marilyn remained in the intensive care unit for five days. No one was able to tell me why Marilyn had had a cardiac arrest. Some had opinions, but no one knew exactly why. An EEG test was done on Marilyn on Sunday November 1. I spoke with Marilyn's neurologist a few days later, and he said, "The EEG test did not reveal any damage. In fact, the episode that she had last May does not even show up. I believe that she's not responding now because her body is so exhausted." He then added, "I believe that she had the cardiac arrest because of her respiratory problem."

Marilyn was transferred to another room after being in the intensive care unit for five days. During the next ten days, Marilyn's condition did not improve much at all. One day I said to one of Marilyn's doctors, "What do you think about Marilyn's condition?" He did not have any positive news at all. I remember saying to him, "Is she just being tortured by all that equipment?"

The doctor answered, "Your wife is fairly young. Let's give it some time."

On two occasions, Marilyn had a substantial amount of fluid removed from her lungs. The respiratory therapist would try to wean Marilyn from the ventilator nearly every day. Marilyn seemed to do well at first, but by late afternoon her breathing was very labored. I remember having the thought one evening, *Please turn that ventilator back on. This is an ugly sight.*

Even though Marilyn's condition did not seem to be improving, God was hearing and answering the many prayers that were being prayed locally and across the country. The Great Physician was about to manifest His healing power.

8

In All Things Give Thanks

Throughout Marilyn's prolonged hospitalization, the Holy Spirit would remind me of the times that He would have me say to my congregation, "In everything give thanks; for this is the will of God in Christ Jesus for you" (1 Thes. 5:18).

I found that it was so much easier to preach that truth than it was to live it. It was very difficult for me to be thankful when my wife was in a coma and breathing with mechanical assistance. It was very difficult for me to be thankful when I was told that my wife was diagnosed with a very rare disease, so rare that there is no known cure and there are only about 150 known cases in the entire world. It was very difficult for me to be thankful when Marilyn's doctors would not be able to give me any positive news about Marilyn's condition. It was very difficult for me to be thankful when I was away from home with no end to Marilyn's hospitalization in sight.

Yet I knew that God wanted me to have a thankful spirit, especially toward Him. In His Word, God talks to us about the sacrifice of praise. "Therefore by Him let us continually offer the sacrifice of praise to God, that is, the fruit of our lips, giving thanks to His name" (Heb. 13:15). It's very easy for us to be thankful to God and to praise Him when all things are well in our lives. However, when everything seems to be going wrong in our lives, it often is a sacrifice for us to offer praise and thanksgiving to God. Only through the help and Person of the Holy Spirit can you offer the sacrifice of praise.

We have a large sign on the church property which faces the highway. The sign is constructed so that we are able to put messages below the church name and service times. After realizing that I needed to have an attitude of thanksgiving even when all things seemed to be going wrong, I put this message on our church signboard when I returned home that week: "In all things give thanks." That message remained on our church signboard throughout Marilyn's hospitalization. I asked God to reveal to me reasons I could have a thankful spirit during that very difficult time. How and why could I offer the sacrifice of praise? God directed me in His Word to Psalm 100.

Why Could I Offer the Sacrifice of Praise?

Psalm 100:3a, "Know that the Lord, He is God."

The Holy Spirit said that one reason that I could be thankful was because God wanted to reveal Himself to me in this very difficult time. God reminded me of Genesis 3:9 where it records God asking Adam, "Where are you?" God certainly knew where Adam was as he was trying to hide from God. I was reminded that God certainly knew where

Marilyn and I were, too. All throughout the Bible we see God revealing Himself to mankind.

In the Old Testament, God revealed Himself to various prophets and enabled them to speak and reveal God's Word to the people. In the New Testament, we read how the Lord Jesus revealed Himself to His first disciples. In Matthew 4:18–22 we read that as Jesus was walking by the Sea of Galilee, He saw Peter and Andrew fishing. Jesus revealed Himself to them and said to them, "Follow Me, and I will make you fishers of men." Later, Jesus saw two other brothers, James and John, in the boat with their father, mending their nets. Jesus revealed Himself to them and immediately they left their boat and father and followed Jesus.

Jesus revealed Himself to the multitudes. He revealed Himself to a man named Nicodemus, and Jesus said, "Unless one is born again, he cannot see the kingdom of God" (John 3:3). Jesus revealed Himself to a short man named Zacchaeus. Zacchaeus wanted to see Jesus as Jesus came through his town, but he had a difficult time because he was very short. So Zacchaeus climbed a tree. However, Jesus saw him in that tree, revealed Himself to Zacchaeus, and said to him, "Zacchaeus, make haste and come down, for today I must stay at your house" (Luke 19:5). The Lord Jesus knew where Zacchaeus was, and He knew his name.

The Lord Jesus revealed Himself to one of the thieves that was crucified next to Him. Jesus said to him, ". . . today you will be with Me in Paradise" (Luke 23:43). I was reminded of God's Word in Revelation 3:20 where Jesus says, "Behold I stand at the door and knock. If anyone hears My voice and opens the door, I will come in to him and dine with him, and he with Me."

I would pray and ask God to reveal Himself to me in this difficult time. I would ask for Him to show me what

He was doing and what He was saying. It was during this time that I received an encouraging card from one of our church members. Melba wrote in her card, "God will bring a blessing out of all this sickness and despair." I began to look for that blessing.

Psalm 100:3*b*, "It is He who made us, and not we ourselves."

I sensed God saying to me that another reason that I could be thankful is that He was in control of the entire situation. The Holy Spirit reminded me again that God created Marilyn's body. He knew what was wrong. He knew what needed to be done. He reminded me once again that He loved Marilyn more than I did or ever could. He reminded me of His Word, "I will praise you, for I am fearfully and wonderfully made; Marvelous are Your works, and that my soul knows very well" (Ps. 139:14). I began to be thankful that God would take control of the entire situation.

Psalm 100:3*c*, "We are His people."

The Holy Spirit reminded me that I could be thankful because I knew that Marilyn belonged to God. I knew that Marilyn was one of His children. I could be thankful that I knew that she was raised in a Christian home and always wanted to do for God what He would have her do.

During Marilyn's hospitalization someone from Marilyn's home church said to me, "I will always remember Marilyn as the nursery girl. She enjoyed working in the nursery." I was reminded of the other different ministries that Marilyn was involved with throughout her life. I began to be thankful for how Marilyn was a part of my ministry and how she complements it in many ways. I began to be thankful that I knew Marilyn would always be with the Lord.

Psalm 100:3*d*, "The sheep of His pasture."

The Holy Spirit reminded me that I could be thankful because I knew that God cared for Marilyn. She was one of His sheep. He reminded me of the parable in Luke 15 where Jesus said, "What man of you having a hundred sheep, if he loses one of them, does not leave the ninety-nine in the wilderness, and go after the one which is lost until he finds it?" God once again reminded me that He knew exactly where Marilyn was because she was one of His. I could be thankful for that fact.

I was once again reminded by the Holy Spirit of that beautiful twenty-fifth wedding anniversary gift that Marilyn gave to me, the Twenty-third Psalm surrounded by a beautiful silver frame. God reminded me that I committed Marilyn to Him. He reminded me of how He spoke to me a few months earlier in the parking lot of a grocery store when Rosie said to me, "Isn't it good to know that we have Jesus to turn to in our time of need?" He reminded me that I could be very thankful because God was holding Marilyn in the palm of His hand.

Psalm 100:5a, "For the Lord is good."

The Holy Spirit reminded me that I could be thankful because God has been and will always be exceedingly good to me. He reminded me of how He was using other people to minister to me and to encourage me during that very difficult time. I began to express thanksgiving to God for my parents and other family members whom I knew were constantly praying for Marilyn. I expressed thanksgiving for my congregation that I was pastor of. I knew that many prayers were being offered to God on behalf of Marilyn and me. I was thankful for those who came to Pittsburgh to visit Marilyn and me. I expressed thanksgiving to God for the very many cards that Marilyn and I received in the mail.

The Holy Spirit reminded me of the special friends that Marilyn and I have and how God was using them to bless and encourage our lives during this difficult time. God reminded me of the very special neighbors that Marilyn and I have. "Big Rude" was taking care of my lawn. His wife, Mary, would make meals for me when I was home. Willard was taking care of our mail and newspaper. His wife, Beryl, would also make meals for me when I was home. Beryl would inform other neighbors and relatives for me concerning Marilyn's condition. Luella came to visit Marilyn several times and would also call and express concern about her. Luella and Margaret made tomato juice for Marilyn and me from the many tomatoes that were still in our garden.

The Holy Spirit reminded me of God's Word, "If you then, being evil, know how to give good gifts to your children, how much more will your Father who is in Heaven give good things to those who ask Him!" (Matt. 7:11). I needed to continue to ask God to be with me and bring healing to Marilyn. The Holy Spirit reminded me that I could be thankful for Marilyn's doctors, nurses, and for Pittsburgh Presbyterian-University Hospital. He reminded me that I could be thankful for the McKee Family House where I stayed. It was only because God blessed many generous people and through their generosity that the Family House became a reality.

I was thankful for the people that I met who were also staying at the Family House. Some of those people were Chris and Maria Witman, Christians from Costa Rica. They prayed a special prayer for Marilyn before they returned home, and they assured me that they would continue to remember Marilyn in their prayers. I was thankful for Chris' mother, who said to me, "Maybe a miracle will happen in Marilyn's life."

I was thankful for Georgie, a fine Christian woman whose husband was dying from cancer. Georgie gave me the toll-free telephone number of the United Methodist twenty-four-hour prayer room. I was thankful for Herb. Herb is from Erie and had been staying at the Family House about six weeks before I came. He was in Pittsburgh to receive daily heart treatments and was also on the heart transplant list. Herb and I shared fishing stories as we sat on the front porch of the Family House, waiting on the shuttle bus for a ride to the hospital.

I was thankful for Barb. Barb had her two small children with her. Her husband was a patient at Presbyterian-University Hospital. He was very ill and waiting for a heart transplant operation. Nearly every day she would express concern for Marilyn. I was thankful for Tom from State College, Pennsylvania. I met him in the hospital's cafeteria one day. His wife had been hospitalized for several weeks. He and I met to eat from time to time.

It didn't take very much effort to notice the goodness of God toward Marilyn and me, even in that very difficult and stressful time. I was reminded that God was good to me in allowing Marilyn to be my wife. I was reminded of God's Word, "He who finds a wife finds a good thing, and obtains favor from the Lord" (Prov. 18:22). God's Word also states, "Who can find a virtuous wife? For her worth is far above rubies" (Prov. 31:10). I'll never forget the first visit of Marilyn's friend Becky and her husband, Ron. It was Saturday September 19. Marilyn had been in a coma for a week. We were sitting in the hospital cafeteria and Becky said, "Guy, I have something for you, and I want you to know that it is from Marilyn." It was bridge-mix candy, which is my favorite kind.

Becky works in a candy store, and a few days prior to Marilyn's hospitalization, Marilyn mentioned to Becky that she would be stopping by soon to purchase bridge mix for me. Becky remembered that and blessed me with that special gift. Tears streamed down my face in the hospital cafeteria that day as I was thankful for a good wife and our friend Becky who remembered and was kind enough to give to me what Marilyn would have if she could.

Psalm 100:5*b*, "His mercy is everlasting."

The Holy Spirit reminded me that I could be thankful because of the mercy of God always will be. He reminded me of Psalm 136, which recounts the mercy of God. Psalm 136:1, "Oh, give thanks to the Lord, for He is good! For His mercy endures forever." The remainder of that chapter speaks of God's creation and also gives us a mini-history of how God took care of His people during the Old Testament days. The last verse of Psalm 136 again states, "Oh, give thanks to the God of heaven! For His mercy endures forever."

The Holy Spirit reminded me of the chorus that we sing in our church at times, "I Will Sing of the Mercies of the Lord," taken from Psalm 89:1. I realized that God was and will always be very compassionate to me and all of His children. I once again was able to sing within myself, *I will sing of the mercies of the Lord*. I was thankful for those that God used to continue to remind me that Marilyn and I were not in this situation alone. God was using people to minister to us and to extend God's compassion and mercy.

Psalm 100:5*c*, "His truth endures to all generations."

The Holy Spirit reminded me that I could be thankful because God has been, and will always be, faithful to His Word. He reminded me of His Word when He spoke to Jacob in the Old Testament in Genesis 28:15–17, "'Behold,

I am with you and will keep you wherever you go, and will bring you back to this land; for I will not leave you until I have done what I have spoken to you.' Then Jacob awoke from his sleep and said, 'Surely the Lord is in this place, and I did not know it.' And he was afraid and said, 'How awesome is this place! This is none other than the house of God, and this is the gate of heaven!'"

God reminded me of what He said in 1 Corinthians 10:13, "No temptation has overtaken you except such as is common to man; but God is faithful, who will not allow you to be tempted beyond what you are able, but with the temptation will also make the way of escape, that you may be able to bear it." I was reminded by the Holy Spirit of the many times that I preached on that verse. I knew that the way of escape was the very presence of God that would enable me, and anyone else who was going through a difficult time, to make it.

I was reminded of what God's Word states in 1 Thessalonians 5:24: "He who calls you is faithful, who will also do it."

And so I learned to offer the sacrifice of praise and thanksgiving to God.

I'll never forget when Marilyn came out of the coma and began to communicate. Many times after one of her nurses or doctors ministered to her, Marilyn would utter the words, "Thank you." Her voice was very weak, and I don't know if her nurses or doctors always heard her, but I heard it loud and clear every time. If Marilyn could utter "thank you" and offer the sacrifice of praise in her weakened state, then there was no reason I could not do the same. I always knew Marilyn had a strong faith in God and His Word, but there was no doubt about that fact to all who were around her as God was beginning the healing process.

Shortly after Marilyn was admitted to Pittsburgh Presbyterian-University Hospital in September of 1998, I was made aware that there was a gospel concert by Bill Gaither and Friends scheduled to be held at 7:00 P.M. on Friday November 13, 1998 in Johnstown, Pennsylvania, at the Cambria County War Memorial.

Marilyn and I watch the Gaither Home Coming Hour nearly every week, and we had attended one of their concerts at the Civic Arena in Pittsburgh, Pennsylvania, in March of 1998. It was a real blessing. When I first was made aware of the scheduled concert, I remember thinking to myself, *That's nearly two months away. Surely Marilyn will be out of the hospital by that time and back to normal.*

On Sunday November 8, following our Sunday morning worship service, our music minister, Bill Gillin, asked me if I had a ticket for the Gaither gospel concert. I told him that I did not. Bill said, "I really think you should go. I think it will do you a lot of good. I know that I could get a ticket for you." I agreed with him that I would receive a blessing by attending the concert and asked him to call me when he had the ticket. The day before the scheduled concert, I received word that a ticket was available. A good friend of ours, Barb Killian, was ill and unable to attend the concert. I was told that her ticket was available. After receiving that ticket I was still reluctant to attend the concert. I thought to myself, *I better not attend that concert. I should stay at Marilyn's bedside.* Marilyn was beginning to be more alert at that time.

I had thought that my mind was made up when the telephone rang in my study. It was our district minister, Rev. Ron Beachley. Bro. Ron asked me, "Do you have a ticket for the Gaither concert tonight?"

I said to him, "God certainly must want me to attend that concert." I did have a ticket, but I was reluctant to attend.

Bro. Ron said, "My wife has an extra ticket. Why don't you consider going and sitting with us? I'll stop by the hospital this afternoon to visit Marilyn, and I'll give you the ticket then." I agreed to meet him at the hospital and to attend the Gaither gospel concert with them. I am so thankful that I did.

9

The Dramatic Manifestation of Divine Healing

I don't think I will ever forget that special Gaither and Friends gospel concert. I know there were many good gospel songs sung that night. However, the one I remember most is the one that Bill Gaither sang as he was introduced to the capacity crowd. Bill Gaither began to sing the chorus to the song "It Is No Secret."

> It is no secret what God can do.
> What He's done for others,
> He'll do for you.
> With arms wide open,
> He'll pardon you.
> It is no secret what God can do.

Tears streamed down my face as Bill Gaither sang that chorus. The presence of God was so very real in that building. I remember thinking to myself, *It is no secret what God can do. God specializes in doing the impossible. Nothing is impossible with God.*

Bill Gaither continued to sing,

There is no night,
for in His light You'll never walk alone.
Always feel at home
wherever you may roam.
There is no power can conquer you,
while God is on your side.
Just take Him at His promise;
Don't run away and hide.*

He then repeated the chorus.

I remember sensing the beautiful peace and presence of God. I remember faith swelling up within me. I remember sensing the Lord saying to me, "It's going to be all right." The Holy Spirit once again reminded me of that beautiful twenty-fifth wedding anniversary gift that Marilyn gave to me, the Twenty-third Psalm surrounded by a beautiful silver frame. I remembered that I committed Marilyn to the Lord. I was thankful that Jesus Christ was my Shepherd and Marilyn's Shepherd. I was thankful that our music minister, Bill Gillin, and our district minister, Rev. Ron Beachley, insisted I attend that concert.

There is no way that I can put in words what I and all of Marilyn's doctors, nurses, therapists, family, and friends were about to begin to witness the following week. Marilyn's condition was about to improve very rapidly as the manifestation of divine healing began.

On November 14, 1998, the day following the Bill Gaither and Friends gospel concert, Marilyn was taken off the ventilator and put on a trachea mask during the day. She was put back on the ventilator at night. She continued

* Words and Music by Stuart Hamblen
Copyright © 1950, 1977 by MCA Music Publishing,
a division of Universal Studios, Inc.
Used by permission.

that way for three more days. On November 17, Marilyn began to eat pureed food. She also sat in a chair for five hours that day. When I entered her room the next day, November 18, the trachea mask was removed, and oxygen had been placed in her nose. I'll never forget Marilyn's physical therapist, Heather. She was Marilyn's physical therapist during her hospitalization in Johnstown. I graduated from high school with her mother, and Heather looked exactly like her. I'll never forget the shocked look of surprise on Heather's face as Marilyn began moving her legs more and more. I'll never forget seeing Marilyn stand up for the first time since her hospitalization. That also occurred on November 18, 1998. The next day, November 19, Marilyn walked twenty steps. What a sense of joy and happiness! The doctors said that Marilyn no longer needed to be on oxygen, and they also removed the trachea tube that day.

I'll never forget the conversation between Marilyn and one of her medical doctors on Friday morning November 20, 1998. She was sitting in a chair that morning as the doctor entered her room. At that time, Marilyn had a feeding tube in her nose and she also still had the catheter. As the doctor was standing next to her he asked, "Marilyn, do you want that tube out of your nose?" Marilyn answered, "What do you think, doctor? Of course I want that tube out of my nose." The doctor replied, "Well, you're going to have to eat really well." Marilyn answered, "I know that I have to eat well. Next week is Thanksgiving Day, and I have to get used to eating good meals. Also, I know that I'll eat much better when I return home."

The doctor seemed to be taken aback. He wanted Marilyn to enter a local rehabilitation center for physical therapy and rehabilitation before she finally went home. Marilyn replied, "I'm not going anywhere but home. The therapists can come to my home, and I can get stronger in my own home."

The doctor seemed to be taken aback again, and he replied, "Mrs. Myers, look at you. When you came here you were in very bad physical condition." He then spoke of the different organs in her body that were very weak at one point. The doctor continued, "Mrs. Myers, look at you now. Thank God," the doctor said emphatically.

Marilyn answered, "Doctor, I know that God is helping me. I am thanking God. But I still want to go home!"

The doctor, still very much taken aback, said to Marilyn, "Well, we'll see."

At that time, the doctor and I had a conversation near the nurses' station. I remember him saying to me, "Let's not say anymore to Marilyn about going to a rehabilitation center. Let's not upset her anymore."

I answered, "You are going to have a very difficult time convincing Marilyn to go to the rehabilitation center. She has already made her decision, and she definitely plans to go to her own home." About that time a representative from the rehabilitation center expressed her concerns to me. She thought that if Marilyn did return home her physical condition would weaken instead of improve. I replied, "I don't know if it will or not. But I know that Marilyn is a fighter and she will do her part if she does return home in a few days."

The representative replied, "Well, if she does not improve at home, we still could have her admitted to the center from your home. If Marilyn does return to her own home, we will keep a close watch on her." I agreed.

I returned to Marilyn's room and said to her, "Since you probably will be going home soon, don't you think we should relocate our bedroom back to the first floor for now?"

Marilyn agreed. She then said to me, "Maybe you can call your father and ask him if he could help you move the furniture." I told her that I already had contacted him and that my father could help me the following day, November 21. We agreed that I would come to her hospital room the next morning to help her with breakfast, then return home to relocate our bedroom to the first floor.

On Saturday morning November 21, 1998, as Marilyn was eating breakfast, one of her doctors entered the room and said to Marilyn, "We can take that catheter out today."

Marilyn thought, *It's about time.*

Marilyn's nurse said, "We'll take it out right after lunch."

Finally, after lunch, Marilyn's catheter was removed. I returned to Marilyn's room about 4:00 P.M. that day. I didn't know at the time that the catheter had just been removed. As Marilyn and I were talking she said to me, "I have to go to the bathroom."

I said, "You have a diaper on. Go in the diaper."

Marilyn said, "I don't want to go in this diaper. What's wrong with you?"

I said, "Ring for your nurse."

The nurse came and Marilyn said, "I have to go to the bathroom." The nurse returned with a bedpan in her hand. Marilyn said to her, "I don't want to sit in that cold pan. I want to go in there." Marilyn was facing the bathroom.

The nurse said, "Are you sure, Marilyn?"

Marilyn said, "Yes, I'm sure." And so Marilyn walked into the bathroom.

After having a catheter for ten weeks, Marilyn surprised her doctors and nurses by not having any trouble urinating at all. Praise be to God! That evening was very special for Marilyn and me. Finally after ten weeks of hospitalization, there were not any tubes or wires connected to Marilyn's body. That evening, as I wheeled her through the hall outside her room, we talked about the possibility of her finally returning to her own home in just a few more days. The Holy Spirit once again reminded me of that very special twenty-fifth wedding anniversary gift from Marilyn, the Twenty-third Psalm surrounded by a beautiful silver frame.

As I was lying in bed Saturday night November 21 at approximately 10:30 P.M., I sensed the Holy Spirit asking me to call my friend Pastor Johnny Bryant in Lake Placid, Florida. I remember thinking, "It's 10:30 P.M. on Saturday night. Johnny is probably in bed by now." I still sensed the Lord telling me to call Johnny, so I did.

Johnny's daughter, Heather, answered the phone. She said, "Daddy's not here right now. He's at the church."

I remember thinking, *What's Johnny doing at the church now? Why isn't he home in bed?*

I immediately called his church office. When Johnny answered the phone, I asked, "Johnny, did you ever see a miracle?"

Johnny said, "What? Why are you asking me that question now?" Johnny seemed taken aback. Why? The Lord had just given Johnny a different message to preach to his congregation the next morning. The title was "The Healing Virtue of Christ." A woman from his congregation had been recently healed of a tumor in her head. Johnny then said, "I was also going to share with my church the change in Marilyn that you told me about a few days ago."

I said, "Johnny, you haven't heard anything yet. Marilyn probably will return to our home on Monday." We both acknowledged that the telephone call at 10:30 P.M. that night and Johnny's new Sunday morning message were from God. We then rejoiced in the goodness of God and His love for His children.

The Sunday morning worship service on November 22 was a very special one for me and for the entire congregation. At prayer time, after receiving prayer requests from the congregation, I asked, "Do you want to hear about Marilyn?"

I heard a resounding, "Yes!" I then reported to the congregation the progress that Marilyn made each day beginning with November 14, 1998 when she was taken off the ventilator during the day. After each day's progress report, I said to the congregation, "Say 'Praise the Lord!'" And they did. When I finally told them that it was very likely that Marilyn would return home the next day, November 23, 1998, the entire congregation applauded. I don't think that I'll ever forget that day. I then reminded the congregation of the special prayer time that we had had together on Sunday September 13, 1998. That was the Sunday that I had asked my friend Rev. Noah Martin to lead our prayer time. During that special prayer time, God spoke to Rev. Martin and had him ask for me to come and kneel at the base of our platform. God then directed Rev. Martin to ask the congregation to come to lay hands on me and to kneel with us in prayer as we cried out to God together for healing and mercy.

After I reminded the congregation of that special prayer time, I said to them, "I need to return to that place today. I invite you to meet with me there again as we thank our Lord for His healing power and mercy." Needless to say, that was also a very special time of prayer. The Holy Spirit reminded me once again of that special twenty-fifth wedding anniversary gift from Marilyn, the Twenty-third Psalm surrounded by a beautiful silver frame.

As I am writing this, I am looking at that beautiful twenty-fifth wedding anniversary gift. Sitting next to it is a beautiful silver plaque that our congregation gave to us as a twenty-fifth wedding anniversary gift. On the plaque is a beautiful cross with two wedding rings on it. Beneath the cross, these words are inscribed: "We are one." Those words remind me of God's Word, "Though one can be overpowered by another, two can withstand him. And a threefold cord is not quickly broken" (Eccles. 4:5).

Oh, how we experienced that truth!

That Sunday afternoon, November 22, 1998, as my parents were preparing to leave Marilyn's room, Marilyn asked my mother, "Are Mark and Diane having Thanksgiving dinner this year?" (Mark is my youngest brother, and he and his wife have had our entire family for Thanksgiving dinner the past several years.)

My mother answered, "Yes, they're having Thanksgiving dinner again this year."

Marilyn replied, "Well, if I don't see you before Thanksgiving Day, I'll see you at Mark and Diane's." We were not sure that would happen, but Marilyn knew that she would be going out for Thanksgiving dinner.

The Miracle Patient Goes Home

As I walked by the nurses' station prior to Marilyn's discharge, one of the nurses stopped me and asked, "Do you know what you wife is known by around here? She is called the 'miracle patient'. When she first came to our floor many of us did not believe that she would walk out of this hospital." She then added, "Isn't God good?" I certainly agreed with her.

We arranged for Marilyn to return home in a transport van. One of the nurses encouraged us to do that because she thought that it would be less stressful for Marilyn and would not require as much energy on her part. Marilyn really wanted to travel home in our own car, but after giving it some thought she agreed to use the transport van. We were told that the van would be at the hospital at 3:00 P.M.

That afternoon was filled with many emotions. Marilyn certainly wanted to go home very badly. I certainly wanted her home. However, we had grown very close to some of her nurses. All of them were so very compassionate and kind to Marilyn. Some of the nurses came by Marilyn's room and said, "We're all going to miss you very much. We really enjoyed having you as a patient."

Marilyn replied, "I'm going to miss you, too. Some day I will stop back to visit with you."

Before Marilyn was discharged, we made arrangements to have a wheelchair, a portable toilet, and a walker sent to our house. Marilyn never did use the wheelchair or the portable toilet. She used the walker for about one week. I will speak more about that in the next chapter.

I'll never forget the day that Marilyn returned home after her ten-week hospitalization. I was anxiously waiting for the transport van. It finally arrived. It was 4:00 P.M., November 23, 1998. As the driver wheeled Marilyn out of the van, some of our neighbors waved at her. Marilyn waved back. She was wearing a great big smile.

The driver helped Marilyn across our living room and to the sofa. I signed the necessary papers for the use of the van and said thanks and goodbye to the driver. When I closed the door and looked at Marilyn, she began to weep and weep. She said to me, "I don't recognize this place."

I answered, "What do you mean you don't recognize this place? This is our home."

I later learned what Marilyn meant by that remark. We had replaced our living room windows a few weeks before Marilyn was hospitalized. We had also purchased and installed new draperies. Marilyn had forgotten about the new windows and drapes. It didn't take very long for her to realize that she was finally home and there is no place like home.

The next few hours were filled with many emotions. Marilyn wanted to see how I had our bedroom set up. It was done to her satisfaction. Our neighbor Luella came over to be with Marilyn while I went to the pharmacy. Before Marilyn was discharged, I had asked her nurse if she would call the pharmacy and order Marilyn's prescriptions for me. She had said that she would. After I had stood in line at the pharmacy for ten minutes, the clerk said to me, "I can't find an order for your wife. Are you sure the nurse called?"

I replied, "She said she was going to call."

The pharmacist heard our conversation and said, "No one called for prescriptions for Marilyn."

I immediately thought, *Maybe she called the wrong pharmacy.* I then called the hospital and asked for Marilyn's nurse. She was not there. Another nurse reached Marilyn's nurse at home. She had forgotten to call in the order for Marilyn before going home. I immediately became anxious because Marilyn needed the prescriptions that night and it was getting close to the pharmacy's closing time. Immediately I felt convicted for worrying. The Holy Spirit reminded me that I had Marilyn's hospital discharge paper in my pocket. It had a list of Marilyn's prescriptions on it. I showed it to the pharmacist, and he filled Marilyn's order. It all worked out. It really doesn't pay to worry. It does pay to trust God and lean on Him.

While I was grocery shopping the next day, I purchased a small turkey. I knew that Marilyn was planning to go to my brother's for Thanksgiving dinner, but we always made a small turkey for ourselves. I brought it home and said to Marilyn, "I bought a turkey." She wanted to know why.

She said, "We're going to Mark and Diane's for Thanksgiving dinner."

I said, "I know we are. However, if you are willing to teach me how to do a turkey, we'll do one for ourselves like we always did."

Marilyn said, "This is going to be fun."

Marilyn is a good teacher. She did teach me how to do a turkey and make the stuffing, and she also taught me how to make gravy. Marilyn said it was good. I know it wasn't as good as hers, but at least it was edible. God's Word states, "And we know that all things work together for good, to those who love God, to those who are the called according to His purpose" (Rom. 8:28). One good thing that was happening during this time was that I was learning how to cook—and even enjoying it.

On Thanksgiving Day, Marilyn and I did go to my brother's for dinner, just as Marilyn said we would. That was a very special Thanksgiving Day. Marilyn ate quite a bit, and she also was able to feed herself the entire meal. She ate all of the traditional Thanksgiving Day food. I was assisting her at mealtime prior to this. Remember, she had just started to eat pureed food eight days earlier.

I had scheduled Marilyn's beautician, Tina, to come to our house the next day, Friday November 27. Marilyn's hair had not been cut for at least three months. When Tina was finished, Marilyn really looked like herself. It also obviously made Marilyn feel so much better.

I'll never forget December 2, 1998. That was Marilyn's first appointment with her local medical doctor since her discharge from the hospital. The doctor was keeping abreast of Marilyn's condition during her hospitalization, but he had not seen her at all. Marilyn walked into the waiting area with the aid of her walker, and one of the nurses said to me, "We were wondering how you were going to get Marilyn in here."

The doctor said, "Look, she's walking in herself."

Once we were in the doctor's office, Marilyn received a big hug from him. The doctor then asked me to tell him about Marilyn's progress. I said, "Doctor, it all began the day our church held an all-day prayer vigil for Marilyn. That day was October 7, 1998." I then continued to tell him what I saw Marilyn go through and what I experienced God do for her.

The doctor looked at Marilyn and said, "Marilyn, you are a miracle—if you believe in miracles. When I last spoke to the people in Pittsburgh, I didn't think that I would ever see you again."

Marilyn replied, "Well, I believe in miracles." Needless to say, that was a special moment.

I also reminded her doctor that when Marilyn was admitted to Pittsburgh Presbyterian-University Hospital on September 10, 1998, she could not see out of the right side of either eye. One of the neurologists said to me that that part of her vision realistically would not return, but he said it could possibly slightly improve. When Marilyn was admitted she could not write her name and she could not fully express herself. The neurologist had shown Marilyn a picture of four garden tools and asked her to tell him the names of the tools. Marilyn began to cry. She said, "I know what they are. I just can't say what they are. Ask my husband. He'll tell you that I know what they are."

Well, her vision not only improved, it was completely restored. Her ability to fully express her thought has also been fully restored. Marilyn's neurologists in Pittsburgh also said that Marilyn's last MRI exam did not reveal any damaged area due to her stroke-like episode. They said, "The MRI exam revealed that that area is fully healed."

In the first chapter of this book I spoke of Marilyn's hospitalization in May of 1998 at the Conemaugh Memorial Hospital in Johnstown. One of the problems that was discovered with Marilyn then was the chordae tendonini. One of the chords holding the mitro valve in her heart had ruptured. The doctor telephoned me at our residence at that time to tell me about that problem. I remember asking him, "Does this mean surgery?"

He replied, "No, not now. Perhaps in a year or two." Marilyn was then placed on a blood thinner. She remained on the blood thinner during the summer of 1998. During Marilyn's hospitalization in Pittsburgh later that year, her doctors there asked me on several occasions why Marilyn was prescribed a blood thinner. I explained the entire situation that had happened to Marilyn in May of 1998. The doctors then asked me for Marilyn's cardiologist's name and telephone number. A few days later the doctors in Pittsburgh said to me, "We are taking Marilyn off the blood thinner. We cannot find anything wrong with her heart valves or the chords holding them in place."

During Marilyn's first visit with her doctor in Johnstown on December 2, 1998, I said to him, "By the way, doctor, what's the scoop with this torn chord around Marilyn's heart valve?"

I'll never forget him looking at me, shaking his head, and saying, "Apparently it has been healed. The tests do not reveal anything wrong." Praise be to God! When our Lord does something, He does it right!

10

The Rose Will Bloom Again

S hortly after Marilyn's hospitalization in Johnstown in May of 1998, friends of ours, George and Alice McDowell, visited with us in our home one Sunday afternoon. One reason they stopped by was that they wanted to inform us about Co Enzyme Q-10. This all-natural liquid is supposed to help maintain healthy heart, circulatory, and immune functions. They gave us an article describing the enzyme in detail.

As they were preparing to leave, George looked at me and said, "Don't worry; the rose will bloom again."

I remember immediately thinking to myself, *Why did he say that? We do have a yellow rosebush in front of our house. Did that cause him to make that remark?* For some reason, those words remained fresh in my mind throughout the summer of 1998: "The rose will bloom again."

Marilyn and I read the article about Co Enzyme Q-10, and Marilyn agreed that she would begin to take it. You can purchase it over the counter, and the very next day I purchased a bottle of this enzyme, and Marilyn began to take it that very day. When the McDowells gave us that article, I remember very well having the thought, *This is from the Lord. God had these people stop here today.*

It was during that time that Marilyn had a rash begin to break out on her body. The rash started at the base of her neck and day by day seemed to move down further on her body. Marilyn was seeing her doctor very frequently at that time. He believed that Marilyn was allergic to one or both of the new medications that were prescribed for her. On one of the visits to the doctor during that time, I gave him the article on Co Enzyme Q-10. After glancing at the article he said, "Marilyn should not be taking something like that. I didn't know that she was taking this." Needless to say, Marilyn did not take any more C-Q-10. However, those words remained with me throughout the summer: "The rose will bloom again."

In sharing this experience, I do not want you to think that I am speaking negatively of Marilyn's doctor. I am not. We think very highly of him, and we know that he is one of the best. He has been Marilyn's doctor since 1985 and has given her excellent care. I am also one of his patients.

Shortly after Marilyn was diagnosed at Pittsburgh Presbyterian Hospital in September of 1998, I was told that Marilyn would be given certain vitamins as well as Co Enzyme Q-10. I remember saying to Marilyn's nurse, "Would you repeat that, please? Did you say Co Enzyme Q-10?"

The nurse answered, "That's what I said." Immediately, I heard those words again in my spirit very loudly and clearly: "The rose will bloom again." The Holy Spirit once again reminded me of the twenty-fifth wedding anniversary gift that Marilyn gave to me, the Twenty-third Psalm surrounded by a beautiful silver frame. I remember thanking God again for being my Shepherd and Marilyn's Shepherd. The Holy Spirit reminded me that I fully committed Marilyn to Him.

I began to search God's Word. Why did Mr. McDowell say those words to me? What was God trying to say to me? The Holy Spirit directed me to Isaiah 35:1–4, "The wilderness and the wasteland shall be glad for them, And the desert shall rejoice and blossom as the rose. It shall blossom abundantly and rejoice, Even with joy and singing. The glory of Lebanon shall be given to it, the excellence of Carmel and Sharon. They shall see the glory of the Lord, the excellency of our God. Strengthen the weak hands, and make firm the feeble knees. Say to those who are fearful-hearted, 'Be strong, do not fear! Behold, your God will come with vengeance, with the recompense of God; He will come and save you.'" The last verse of that chapter states, "And the ransomed of the Lord shall return, and come to Zion with singing, with everlasting joy on their heads. They shall obtain joy and gladness, and sorrow and sighing shall flee away."

During Marilyn's hospitalization in Pittsburgh, I would return to Johnstown about twice a week. During the three weeks that Marilyn was in a coma, several things happened that reminded me again of those words: "The rose will bloom again."

One day a neighbor said to me, "The roses on your rosebush are so beautiful. Why don't you take some back to Pittsburgh and put them in Marilyn's room?" The next day I did put some beautiful blooming roses in Marilyn's room and also some in my room at the Family House. When I looked at those roses I would be reminded of George McDowell's words: "The rose will bloom again."

About a week later, while I was at Willard and Beryl's house to get my mail, Beryl said, "Look at this beautiful picture. Take this back to Pittsburgh with you and put it in Marilyn's room." She had taken a picture of our yellow rosebush that is in the front of our house. Once again those words echoed in my spirit: "The rose will bloom again."

I remember saying to Beryl, "Why don't you keep this picture here with you? We can show it to Marilyn when she becomes conscious." I remember calling Beryl on the telephone a few days after Marilyn returned to her own home, and I said to her, "Beryl, if you have a minute come over and show Marilyn that beautiful picture that you took of all the blooming roses on our rosebush."

She replied, "I'll be right over."

That was a special day. As Beryl and Marilyn were talking about that picture, I was admiring the beautiful yellow rose that our neighbor Luella gave Marilyn a few days before Marilyn was discharged. That rose was the last one of the season from Luella's own rosebush. My "rose," Marilyn, was finally home and on her way to a full recovery.

The first few weeks that Marilyn was home were very busy for us. Nurses came to our house twice a week to monitor Marilyn's progress. They all were very kind and caring. Nearly every time that they came they remarked and marveled about Marilyn's progress. I remember one nurse saying to Marilyn, "Marilyn, when I read your chart and all that happened to you, I said to myself, 'This woman must weigh at least 300 pounds for her body to be able to tolerate all that she went through.'" Marilyn had a doctor's appointment today, January 13, 1999, and her weight was 98 pounds.

A therapist came to evaluate Marilyn's condition. Soon after that, a physical therapist and an occupational therapist were scheduled to come to our home. The physical therapist, George, came once a week. On George's first visit, Marilyn's feet and leg muscles were so weak that she could not stand on her toes. George gave Marilyn five leg exercises to do until his next visit. He was very pleased with Marilyn's progress. His third visit was his last; that was December 15, 1998. He said, "Marilyn, you are doing very well. You've come a long way in such a short time. I recommend that you speak with your doctor about having outpatient therapy. You really are doing well."

Those words that Mr. McDowell spoke in May of 1998 rang out in my ears: "The rose will bloom again."

Marilyn's home occupational therapist, Christine, also was very pleased with Marilyn's progress. Her last home visit was December 28, 1998. She also recommended that Marilyn talk to her doctor about having outpatient therapy.

After Marilyn returned home, so many things happened that reminded me of those words: "The rose will bloom again." Every time I was reminded of those words, I believed that the Great Physician was speaking to me that He was completing the healing process He had begun in Marilyn's body.

Marilyn returned home on November 23, 1998. The following Sunday, November 29, she was in church. Marilyn and I will never forget the looks on the faces of many of the people as they entered the church vestibule that day and saw Marilyn sitting near the encouragement table. You just had to be there. Following the morning worship service, our youth and pioneer groups sponsored the Second Annual Thanksgiving Dinner. The youth and older children prepared the dinner as a way of saying "Thank You" to the congregation for their prayers and support during the year.

Marilyn and I attended the dinner. During the dinner, Marilyn and Debbie Karla gave Marilyn a special gift. It was a beautiful homemade angel pin. The angel was made of a dark red material with a golden halo and trim. Below the face of the angel, in the middle of a ribbon of gold, was a budding red rose. I couldn't believe it. Marilyn really likes angels. She has quite a collection of various kinds and shapes. God's Word states that "angels are ministering spirits sent forth to minister for those who will inherit salvation" (Heb. 1:14). When our daughter, Melissa, was alive, we often referred to her as "a little angel sent from God." When I saw that beautiful gift, chills went up and down my arms. I was once again reminded of that beautiful twenty-fifth wedding anniversary gift that Marilyn gave to me, and I also heard those words again: "The rose will bloom again." I was so thankful that Marilyn was out of the hospital and able to attend church the very first Sunday that she was home. The rose really was blooming again. Marilyn was on her way to full recovery.

On Saturday December 5, 1998, my father and I went deer hunting. My mother came to our house that day to be with Marilyn until I returned home. When I returned home, I quickly noticed that my mother had washed, colored, and styled Marilyn's hair. We were talking about how good Marilyn was doing and how good she looked when my mother reminded me that there was a message on our answering machine. I quickly listened to the message. The message was from our neighbor, Mary. She said, "I want to draw your attention to your rosebush. There's a beautiful rosebud blooming." (It had been unusually warm in western Pennsylvania at that time.)

When I heard that message, once again chills went up and down my arms. I said to myself, *Thank You, Jesus*. I knew that there was more than one rosebud blooming in western Pennsylvania on December 5, 1998. I knew that the Great Physician was completing the healing process that He started in Marilyn's body.

On December 9, 1998, Marilyn and I attended the annual Conemaugh Valley Community Christmas Choir Festival. Before praying the opening prayer, the pastor said to the congregation, "Marilyn Myers is in attendance here tonight. Isn't the Lord good?" I heard a resounding "Amen" from the congregation. (I think that Marilyn was on nearly every prayer chain in Johnstown.) My little rosebud was blooming. Marilyn was continually improving.

I'll always remember Monday December 14, 1998. My father and I were deer hunting again that day. My mother was staying with Marilyn until I returned home. My father and I returned home early from hunting that day, and I'm so glad we did. I returned home just in time to be there when Marilyn's nurse, Ruth Ann, came to examine her. After Ruth Ann examined Marilyn, she remarked about how well Marilyn was progressing and on how good Marilyn's appearance was. With a big smile on her face, and in the presence of both my mother and me, Ruth Ann looked at Marilyn and said, "You're just like a little blooming rosebud!"

With chills running up and down my arms, I immediately looked at my mother and said, "Did you hear what Ruth Ann just said?" My mother smiled and nodded her head in the affirmative. I later explained to Ruth Ann what we were referring to. Marilyn was released from home nursing on December 22, 1998.

By the way, Ruth Ann called Marilyn last Wednesday evening, January 6, 1999. She said to Marilyn, "I really think about you so much. I just got a new study Bible, and as I was looking through it tonight I was thinking of you. I want to come visit you some weekend." Marilyn assured Ruth Ann that she was welcome at any time.

My mother teaches piano and organ lessons in her home. A daughter of one of the x-ray technicians that administered a test to Marilyn while she was hospitalized in Johnstown takes piano lessons from my mother. This technician always asked about Marilyn when she brought her daughter for lessons. During the 1998 Christmas season, this technician gave a special gift to my mother. It was a beautiful, ceramic red rose. Immediately my mother told her that I was writing a book about Marilyn's illness and healing and the name of the last chapter. The technician replied, "I'm getting chills on my arms."

The Christmas season in 1998 was very special for Marilyn and me. We were not involved in all the hustle and bustle of the commercialization of Christmas. We were rejoicing in the fact that on that very first Christmas day, God manifested Himself in the flesh by sending us the Lord Jesus Christ. That's what Christmas is all about. We were also rejoicing in the fact that the Lord Jesus, the Great Physician, manifested His divine healing power in Marilyn's body.

A few days before Christmas, Marilyn asked me to take her to one of our local Christian bookstores. She remembered that she had ordered a Christmas gift for me several weeks before her hospitalization. When we entered the store, immediately the sales clerks greeted Marilyn with lots of smiles and hugs. They were so glad to see her. The clerks had been praying for Marilyn every morning during their prayer time together. When the hugs were over, Marilyn looked at me and said, "Will you please get lost!" The clerks really enjoyed that. Marilyn wanted to purchase the gift that she had ordered many weeks ago.

Following our Christmas Eve worship service, Marilyn and I returned to our home just to be alone and celebrate Christmas together. We had always given each other gifts on Christmas Eve following the worship service. I gave Marilyn my gift to her. It was a wooden plaque that has these words printed on it: "Angels Gather Here." Marilyn smiled when she opened it and asked me to place it near her angel display on our living room windowsill. Marilyn then gave my gift to me. On the front of the shirt are printed these words beneath a picture of a fisherman: "I'm hooked on Jesus." We both acknowledged the presence of God, for we both really are hooked on Jesus, and we do know that angels really do gather around us to minister to us and to protect us. Why? Because we are God's children and the Lord Jesus really is our Shepherd.

We spent much of Christmas day at my sister's home. Most of my family was there for Christmas dinner. We all were rejoicing over what the Great Physician was doing on behalf of Marilyn. Later that evening Marilyn's brother, Ron, his wife, Jane, and their son, Mark, and daughter, Kris, came to our house to visit with us.

On December 28, 1998, exactly five weeks after Marilyn was discharged from the hospital, she went shopping at the Galleria Mall here in Johnstown. Marilyn wanted to purchase a new pair of shoes. As she got out of our vehicle and walked into the mall by herself, unassisted by me or anyone else, I watched her walking and said to myself, *There goes my beautiful, blooming rose.* I thanked God for being our Great Physician. That evening, my friend Pastor Jack Rupert and his wife invited Marilyn and me to their home. As we sat around the Ruperts' kitchen table, Marilyn was talking and laughing and just having a good time with others. (Do you remember the dream that Pastor Jack had? I wrote about it in chapter 2.)

A few days later I stopped at a local McDonald's for a cup of coffee on my way to the church office. As I was walking out of the restaurant, I heard someone call, "Mr. Myers! Mr. Myers!" I stopped and turned to see who it was. It was one of the medical doctors that treated Marilyn during her hospitalization in Johnstown. The doctor asked, "How's your wife?" With a big smile on my face, I told her just how well Marilyn was doing. The doctor smiled and said, "God's so good." I agreed with her and also thanked her for also giving Marilyn excellent care. As I was driving to the church, I also expressed my thanks to the Great Physician.

On January 13, 1999, Marilyn and I ate lunch at the food court at the Johnstown Galleria Mall. As I was ordering our food, our district minister's wife, Linda, noticed me and asked, "How's Marilyn doing?"

I replied, "She's doing real good. She's sitting right over there."

Linda then said, "It was so good to hear her talking and laughing as we were sitting around our table on New Year's Day." (Do you remember the dreams that my friends Pastor Jack and Pastor Johnny had? I wrote about them in chapter 2.)

I was walking through the Conemaugh Memorial Hospital on that same day. I was there to visit my good friend and neighbor Pete who had had surgery. One of the occupational therapists during Marilyn's hospitalization recognized me and asked, "Is your wife back in the hospital?"

I replied, "No, she isn't, thank God. Marilyn is doing very well." I then elaborated on Marilyn's progress.

The therapist smiled and said, "That's wonderful. I'm so happy for you and your wife." As I continued on my way, I expressed thanksgiving to my Shepherd, the Great Physician, the Lord Jesus Christ.

I took a coffee break as I was in the process of writing this chapter. I glanced at today's edition of our local newspaper as I was enjoying my coffee, and a local store ad immediately caught my attention. The name of the store was Secondhand Rose. A picture of a rosebud was placed near the store name. Beneath the store name was this sentence: "Name Brands with Precious Experience!" This store obviously sold quality secondhand clothes.

The Holy Spirit reminded me that God is a God of new beginnings. Even though Marilyn's prolonged hospital stay was very stressful and troubling, it was also a precious experience. Why? It was a precious experience because the Lord Jesus Christ, the Good Shepherd and Great Physician, revealed Himself to Marilyn, me, and others in a very special way. I would not want to relive that experience for anything in the world, but I also would not trade it for anything in the world. I was also reminded of this scripture when I read that ad: "To him the doorkeeper opens, and the sheep hear his voice; and he calls his own sheep by name and leads them out" (John 10:3).

The Lord Jesus knows your name. He knows where you are right this very minute, and He knows all about your needs. All you have to do is call on His name. He will answer you and minister to you. He will lead you out of your desert places today. It is my prayer and Marilyn's prayer that all who read about this, our precious experience with the Great Physician, would know Jesus Christ as Lord and Savior of their life. It is our prayer that you would have a precious experience with the Lord Jesus.

God also specializes in new beginnings. Nearly every person we read about in God's Word had a new beginning with God. Perhaps you need a new beginning with Him. Ask Him for it. He will give one to you. You can trust Him! You can depend on Him! His promises are true and are available to all who will reach out and receive them.

Marilyn and I are rejoicing in the goodness of God today. The Lord has blessed us in so many ways. Marilyn received a good report during her visit to her doctor on January 13, 1999. Her doctor said, "Marilyn, you are looking better each time. I can see that you're getting stronger." By the way, Marilyn did talk to her doctor about having outpatient therapy. Her doctor said, "It's not so important as to where you exercise, just so you exercise. I can tell that you're getting stronger." Marilyn does exercise her muscles at home by lifting weights and by doing various leg exercises her home physical therapist recommended. After receiving approval from Marilyn's doctor, we purchased airline tickets to Florida. My friend's daughter, Heather Bryant, is getting married on February 6, 1999, and I have the privilege of officiating at the service. I'm sure that Marilyn and I will sit around the Bryants' kitchen table with them. I'm also sure that Marilyn will talk and laugh and just have a good time with the Bryants. (Do you remember the dream that Pastor Bryant had?) Great things happen when God's people are united. Marilyn and I will be eternally grateful to all for the many, many prayers prayed on her behalf.

Our desert, wasteland, and wilderness are rejoicing and blossoming as a rose. They are blossoming abundantly with joy and singing. The weak hands have been strengthened. The feeble knees have been made firm. The fearful-hearted have become strong. We certainly have seen the glory and the excellency of our God. Praise His name forever.

As I was driving to the hospital today, I was listening to a cassette tape by Bill Gaither and Friends. On that tape someone sings a song entitled "Roses Will Bloom Again."

I planted a little rosebush.
I tended it with care.
Its buds began to blossom,
Their sweet fragrance filled the air.
But the winter came and it withered.
The petals drooped and fell to the ground.
My heart sank and it faded.
But I had forgotten who had made it.
He said, "Roses will bloom again.
Just wait and see.
Don't worry about what might have been.
Only God knows how it will end.
Roses will bloom again."*

By the way, I need to add that Marilyn and I recently returned home from our trip to Lake Placid, Florida. What a wonderful time we had as we were guests in the home of our friends Pastor Johnny and Sandy Bryant.

One of the very first things I noticed was the sign on the property of the church that Johnny pastors, Lake Placid First Assembly of God. The sign read, "Come and hear the healing testimony of Marilyn and Guy Myers, 10:45 A.M. and 6:00 P.M. Sunday February 7."

As we then entered the Bryants' house, I noticed that Sandy had their dining room table decorated so beautifully. The silverware was wrapped in white napkins. On each napkin was a beautiful red rosebud. Johnny and Sandy did not know about this chapter of the book and all the reasons for it. Isn't God so good to His children? I told them about the contents of this chapter and that I needed to write about Sandy's special napkins.

* Words and Music by Marcia Henry
  Copyright © 1991 by Marcia Henry Music
  All rights controlled by Gaither Copyright Management
  Used by permission.

Marilyn and I had a great time together with the Bryants that week. It was a real treat and a blessing to be able to officiate at Heather's wedding service. She was such a beautiful bride. I also enjoyed ministering at the 10:45 A.M. and 6:00 P.M. worship services at Johnny's church. His congregation was thrilled to see Marilyn, as they had fasted and prayed for her healing. And we did sit around Johnny and Sandy's dining room table, and we talked and laughed with my "blooming rosebud," Marilyn.

I will always remember the week of November 15, 1998, the week that the Great Physician revealed His healing power in Marilyn's body. One day that week I said to one of Marilyn's doctors as he was standing at her bedside, "What do you think of my miracle girl, doctor?"

He uttered something in the Hebrew language.

I said, "What does that mean?"

The doctor replied, "She has resurrected!"

To order additional copies of

TOUCHED
BY THE
GREAT
PHYSICIAN

AN ACCOUNT OF DIVINE HEALING

send $10.95 plus $3.95 shipping and handling to

Books Etc.
P.O. Box 4888
Seattle, WA 98104

or have your credit card ready and call

(800) 917-BOOK